Weetabix

Book of the
MILLENNIUM
Volume 4: 1901–2000

from the publishers of
The **HUTCHINSON**
ENCYCLOPEDIA

Helicon

First published for Weetabix Limited in Great Britain in 2000 by
Helicon Publishing Ltd
42 Hythe Bridge Street
Oxford OX1 2EP
e-mail address: admin@helicon.co.uk
Web site: http://www.helicon.co.uk

The Weetabix name and logo are the registered trade marks of Weetabix Limited.

Typesetting by Tech Type, Abingdon, Oxon
Layout and design by Norton Matrix Limited, Bath
Printed in Italy by De Agostini, Novara
ISBN: 1-85986-328-0

British Library Cataloguing in Publication Data

A catalogue record for this book is available from the British Library.

Papers used by Helicon Publishing Ltd are natural recyclable products
made from wood grown in sustainable forests. The manufacturing
processes of both raw material and paper conform to the environmental
regulations of the country of origin.

Contributors and Advisors

Ian Crofton	Susan Mendelsohn
Bernadette Crowley	Nigel Seaton
Susan Cuthbert	Cath Senker
Giles Hastings	Andrew Solway
Maggy Hendry	Lisa Sullivan
Louise Jones	Sarah Wearne
Brenda Lofthouse	Christine Withers

Editorial and Production

Editorial Director
Hilary McGlynn

Production
Tony Ballsdon

Managing Editor
Katie Emblen

Picture Research
Elizabeth Loving

Project Managers
Robert Snedden
Lisa Sullivan

Cartography
Olive Pearson

Art and Design
Terence Caven

Editors
Rachel Minay
Edith Summerhayes

Contents

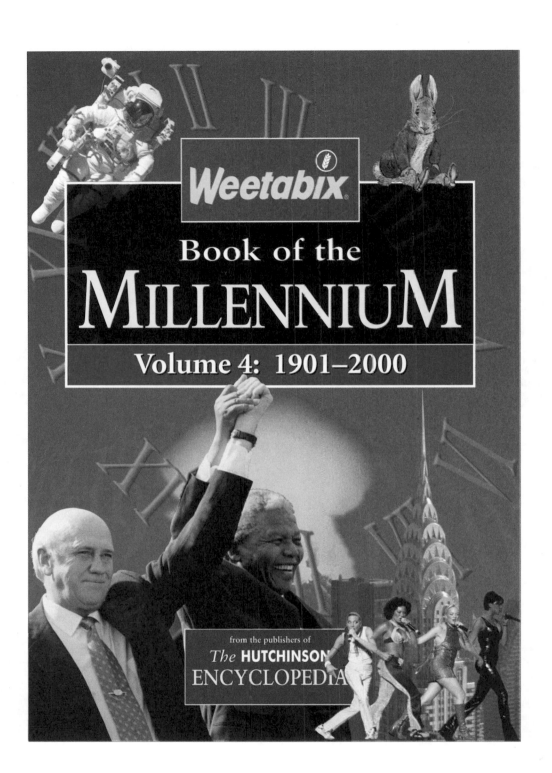

Weetabix

Book of the
MILLENNIUM
Volume 4: 1901–2000

from the publishers of
The **HUTCHINSON**
ENCYCLOPEDIA

The World 1901–2000

1950s

US minister Martin Luther King begins the civil rights movement in the USA.

1914

World War I breaks out in Europe. 8 million lives are lost by the end of the war in 1918.

1969

US astronaut Neil Armstrong becomes the first 'man on the moon'.

1945

World War II ends with the defeat of Nazi Germany.

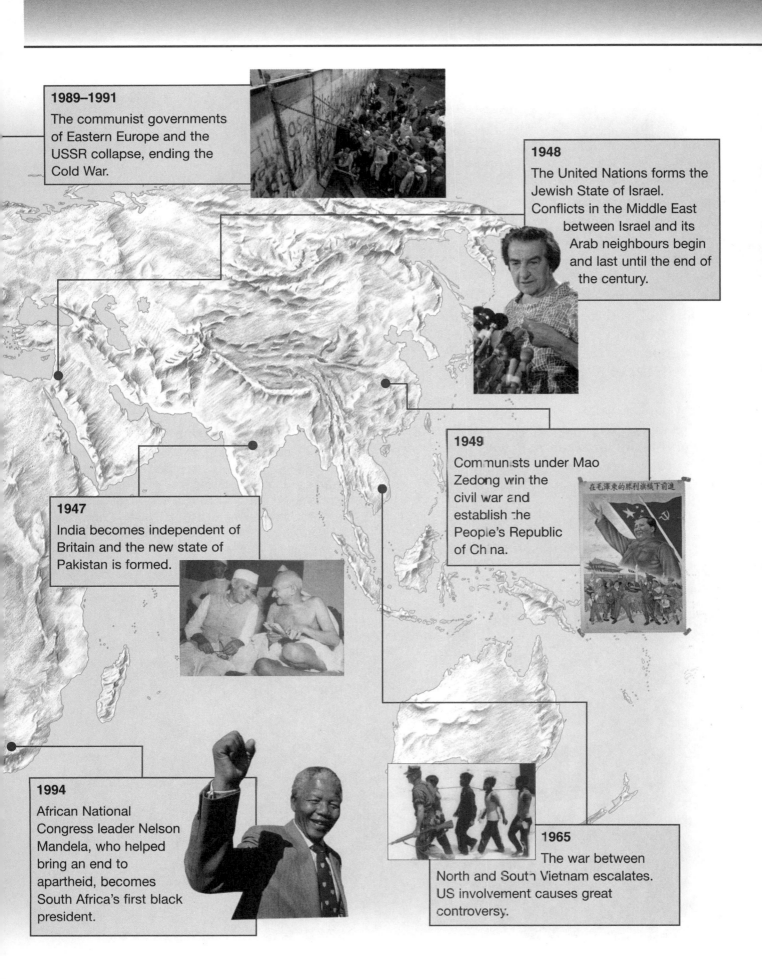

1989–1991

The communist governments of Eastern Europe and the USSR collapse, ending the Cold War.

1948

The United Nations forms the Jewish State of Israel. Conflicts in the Middle East between Israel and its Arab neighbours begin and last until the end of the century.

1949

Communists under Mao Zedong win the civil war and establish the People's Republic of China.

1947

India becomes independent of Britain and the new state of Pakistan is formed.

1994

African National Congress leader Nelson Mandela, who helped bring an end to apartheid, becomes South Africa's first black president.

1965

The war between North and South Vietnam escalates. US involvement causes great controversy.

World War I

What Caused the War?

People at the time blamed Germany for starting World War I. Later, historians suggested that several factors played a part – nationalism (loyalty to a country), imperialism (empire building), militarism, (importance of the armed forces in the way a country is run) and the series of military alliances among the European nations. Some people think that the situation in Europe – many proud nations with large armed forces ready for action – was an explosive mixture waiting for a spark to set it off.

Soldiers shelter in a trench during a lull in the fighting.

Map Legend

Central Powers
Allies
neutral state

Map labels: NORWAY, SWEDEN, North Sea, DENMARK, UNITED KINGDOM, NETHERLANDS, GERMANY, Brest-Litovsk, BELGIUM, ATLANTIC OCEAN, Verdun, LUXEMBOURG, RUSSIA, SWITZERLAND, AUSTRIA-HUNGARY, FRANCE, ITALY, PORTUGAL, SPAIN, Sarajevo, SERBIA, ROMANIA, Black Sea, BULGARIA, ALBANIA, Gallipoli, OTTOMAN EMPIRE, GREECE, Mediterranean Sea

Trench Warfare

One of the main reasons why so many men were killed in World War I was the military technology available at that time. Defenders were always in a much stronger position. They could dig themselves deep trenches and underground 'dugouts' in which they would be safe from bombardments by enemy artillery (heavy guns). In front of the trenches they laid great tangles of barbed wire. When the attacking troops advanced across the 'no man's land' between the opposing trenches, they were caught on the barbed wire, and shot down by the defenders' machine guns and artillery. Various new weapons, such as poison gas, tanks, and aeroplanes, were developed to break down defences, but in the end it was the side that had the greatest resources of men, food, and weapons that won.

The assassination of Franz Ferdinand, the heir to the Austro-Hungarian throne, in Sarajevo on 28 June 1914 provided the spark that led to the outbreak of war. By early August, Germany and Austria-Hungary (the Central Powers) were at war with Britain, France, Belgium, and Russia (the Allies). On the Western Front, fierce fighting by French and British troops prevented the Germans achieving their aim of winning within 42 days. By November the two armies had dug trenches, deep open tunnels in the ground, facing each other from the English Channel to Switzerland. For four years both sides tried to advance, but the front line moved very little, despite millions of deaths.

In April 1915 the British attempted to knock Turkey, Germany's ally, out of the war by attacking the Turks in Gallipoli, a peninsula guarding the route to the Black Sea. The attempt failed. In 1915 Italy entered the war on the side of the Allies and Bulgaria joined the Central Powers. In February 1916 the Germans began a massive attack on the French fortress of Verdun. More than 500,000 French soldiers were killed before the battle ended in December.

War around the World

Although most of the fighting during World War I was in Europe, it involved many people from other continents. Soldiers from the distant parts of the British Empire, such as New Zealand, Australia, South Africa, India, and Canada, came to join Britain's war effort. Similarly, France brought many troops from its African colonies. Later on, the USA, Brazil, some Central American states, and even China and Japan joined in on the side of the Allies. There was submarine warfare all over the Atlantic Ocean, naval battles off Chile and the Falkland Islands, and fighting in the Indian Ocean. The British also attacked the Turkish Ottoman Empire in Palestine and Mesopotamia (modern Iraq), and Allied forces invaded and captured German colonies in Africa and the Pacific.

To help them the British launched an attack on the Somme. On the first day alone, 1 July 1916, over 60,000 British soldiers were killed or injured. Battles like this continued for another two years.

The End of the War

The Germans won a series of victories against the Russians. Defeat, and revolution at home, led the Russians to make peace with Germany at Brest-Litovsk in March 1918. The arrival of US troops in April 1918 turned the tide in favour of Britain and France. Eventually a combination of hunger, political unrest, and military defeats convinced the Germans that they were beaten. An armistice was signed on 11 November 1918, and both sides stopped fighting. Over 8 million men had been killed in the 'war to end all wars'.

The first tanks appeared on the battlefields of World War I.

War and the People of Britain

Posters like this encouraged men to join the army and fight in the war.

'Your Country Needs YOU'

News of the outbreak of war on 4 August 1914 was greeted in Britain by cheering crowds. Men rushed to join the army fearing that the fighting might be over by Christmas. Between August 1914 and December 1915 almost 2½ million men volunteered. This was the first people's army in the history of Britain. They were encouraged by posters persuading them to fight for 'King and Country', or shaming them into wondering what their children might think if they did not. By January 1916 too many men had died in terrible circumstances. The army was getting short of people, so conscription was introduced, requiring all fit men over 18 to join the army.

War Poetry

The early enthusiasm for the war was captured in the poetry of Rupert Brooke, who died of blood poisoning in April 1915. Julian Grenfell, killed in May 1915, wrote of the joy of fighting in his poem 'Into Battle'. By 1916 the realities of war were influencing poets like Siegfried Sassoon, who wrote angrily of stinking bodies and pointless attacks. Perhaps the most famous poetry of this type came from Wilfred Owen, killed one week before the war ended, who described such things as brain-splattered faces and the 'froth-corrupted lungs' of gas victims.

Did You Know?

Poppy seeds can lie dormant (not grow) for many years under the ground. When shellfire churned up the battlefields of France and Flanders (Belgium) it brought millions of poppy seeds to the surface. These flowered thickly all over the devastated landscape. The flower became associated with the war dead. In Britain artificial poppies are worn every year for Remembrance Day, the anniversary of the end of the war on 11 November. Money raised by their sale goes to help disabled servicemen and women.

British soldiers with captured, wounded German soldiers.

Women at War

Some women trained as nurses, while others drove ambulances or joined the Voluntary Aid Detachment (VAD) and became assistant nurses. As more men joined the army, women took over the jobs they had left. Women became bank clerks, grave diggers, bus conductors, or agricultural labourers. Now that it was necessary, women did jobs that were once considered totally unsuitable for them. They were especially important in factories where tanks, aeroplanes, weapons, and explosives were made.

Propaganda

People in Britain never had a very good idea of what was happening at 'the Front'. This was because newspapers were forbidden to mention facts that the authorities did not want the public to know. Propaganda, the presentation of information in such a way as to influence public opinion, was published to keep people misinformed. The propaganda only told people about victories, never the truth about defeats.

Food Shortages and Flu

There were shortages of food and fuel, which by the end of the war were rationed to make sure everyone received a fair share. This prevented the population from starving. Nothing, however, could spare them from the ravages of the Spanish flu epidemic that swept the world in the autumn of 1918. This disease killed more people than were killed in the whole war.

Women had to take on jobs that were normally done by the men who had gone off to fight.

The Unknown Warrior

Over 722,000 British soldiers were killed in the war. One was chosen for burial in Westminster Abbey in London (where many great British people are buried) as a mark of respect to them all. His identity was unknown – he could have been anyone's husband, brother, father, or son. Four unidentified bodies were dug up from four different battlefields and placed in individual coffins. A blindfolded officer touched one of the coffins. This coffin was transported to England on a battleship, then carried by special train to Victoria Station. There it was placed on a gun carriage which led a huge parade through vast crowds to Westminster Abbey. In the presence of King George V, senior military officers, politicians, and representatives from the families of the dead, the coffin was buried inside the Abbey, under earth brought from the battlefields. The dedication on the stone slab covering it began: 'Here lies the body of a British warrior, unknown by name or rank, brought from France to lie amongst the most illustrious [famous] in the land'.

Peacemaking after the War

If the war of 1914 to 1918 was fought to end all wars, as people hoped, the peace treaties needed to be done properly – to create a new world in which everlasting peace was possible.

The Paris Peace Conference

Woodrow Wilson, the US president, arrived in Paris for the Peace Conference with his 'Fourteen Points' for peace, which were intended to be fair to all sides and to establish a peace that would last. The people of Europe, who had suffered so badly from four years of war, were not keen to follow them. The British, French, and Belgian people wanted revenge, and the French in particular wanted to make sure Germany could never threaten them again.

The war caused the collapse of the old Austro-Hungarian, Russian, and Ottoman (Turkish) empires. Many small states took this opportunity to establish their freedom and independence. Woodrow Wilson believed in self-determination, the right of all nations to chose how they wanted to be governed. But which people would make up which nation and where exactly would the state borders be fixed? Such questions were the cause of endless arguments, some of which were still not settled at the end of the 20th century.

The League of Nations

The League of Nations, a world assembly to which each nation sent representatives, was set up in Geneva, Switzerland. International disputes were to be settled here before they led

> ### The Peace Treaties
>
> The Allies made separate treaties with each of the defeated Central Powers:
>
> | | | |
> |---|---|---|
> | 28 | June 1919 | Treaty of Versailles with Germany |
> | 10 | September 1919 | Treaty of Saint-Germain with Austria |
> | 27 | November 1919 | Treaty of Neuilly with Bulgaria |
> | 4 | June 1920 | Treaty of Trianon with Hungary |
> | 10 | August 1920 | Treaty of Sèvres with Turkey |

The leaders of the four major allied countries met at Versailles.

> ### Did You Know?
>
> Many new countries were created as a result of the war, including:
>
> - from the Russian empire: Finland, Latvia, Lithuania, Estonia, and part of Poland;
>
> - from the Austro-Hungarian empire: Austria, Hungary, Czechoslovakia, Yugoslavia, and another part of Poland;
>
> - from the Turkish Ottoman empire: Iraq, Transjordan, Palestine (all administered by Britain after the war), Syria, Lebanon (administered by France after the war), Saudi Arabia (created in 1925), Yemen, and Turkey.

to war. Although the idea was President Wilson's, the American people did not want to join, and eventually other nations saw no reason to obey the League or even to bother with it.

The signing of the peace treaty in the Hall of Mirrors at Versailles.

The Treaty of Versailles

Germany lost Alsace and Lorraine to France, northern Schleswig to Denmark, parts of Silesia and Prussia to Poland, part of East Prussia to Lithuania, the Sudetenland to Czechoslovakia, Malmédy and Eupen to Belgium, and all the German colonies. In addition, the Saar and Rhineland areas of Germany were to be occupied by Allied troops for 15 years. The German army was reduced in size and had to surrender its weapons, and the navy had to give up all its submarines and most of its ships. Germany was not allowed to keep its airforce. The Germans were accused of being the aggressors, causing the war, and were fined £6.6 billion to pay for the damage they had caused. The Germans claimed that the invasion of France and Belgium in 1914 had not been an act of aggression but of self-defence. They felt very angry at being blamed for the war and deeply resented all the terms of the treaty. This resentment was to be a major cause of World War II, 20 years later.

The Russian Revolution

Causes of Revolution in Russia

In 1917 there was a revolution in Russia that led to the creation of the Union of Soviet Socialist Republics (USSR or Soviet Union) in 1922. The revolutionaries took the name Communist Party of the USSR and ruled until its collapse in 1991.

In 1917 over three-quarters of Russians were poor peasants living extremely hard lives in small villages. Tsar Nicholas II (the emperor) was a very harsh ruler, who gave the people little say in running the country. Life had got worse for the ordinary people since the outbreak of World War I in 1914, and many people in Russia wanted an end to the war. Between 1914 and the end of 1916, over 7 million Russian soldiers had died or been injured fighting the Germans and Austrians, and there was no sign of victory or of an end to the conflict. The war had damaged the economy too, and there were widespread food shortages.

The Revolutions of 1917

There were two revolutions in Russia in 1917. The first took place in March, although it is called the February Revolution because it was February in the old Russian calendar. The second revolution took place in November, but is known as the October Revolution for the same reason.

In the February Revolution a democratic provisional government took power from the Tsar. But it could not solve Russia's enormous problems, and did no better in fighting the war. The peasants were taking land from the landowners, soldiers were leaving the army, and there were many strikes.

The Bolsheviks were Communists who wanted another revolution. They believed that soviets – workers' councils in the factories – with the support of the peasants, could take over the economy and run the country. By November 1917 the soviets had become more powerful than the government, and the Bolsheviks started another revolution and seized power.

Peace with Germany and Civil War

In March 1918 Russia made peace with Germany at the Treaty of Brest-Litovsk. The price was high – Russia handed over a large amount of territory, including valuable farmland and industry, together with 60 million people, to the Germans. The treaty was cancelled by the Allies in November 1918.

Between 1918 and 1920 there was a civil war. The people who were against the revolution, the Whites, were backed by forces from 14 foreign countries, including Britain, France, the USA, Japan, and Germany.

The Bolsheviks attack the Tsar's Winter Palace during the 1917 revolution.

The Bolshevik Red Army, led by Leon Trotsky, managed to beat the Whites, but at a huge cost – millions of people died in the civil war.

Outcome of the October Revolution

Following the October Revolution many parts of the old Russian empire, such as Ukraine, Georgia, Armenia, and Azerbaijan, declared their independence. In these places the people were not Russian, and had for a long time disliked Russian domination. However, during the civil war the Bolsheviks reconquered most of these territories, and in 1922 they became republics of the newly founded USSR.

After the October Revolution the Bolshevik government set about making major changes to society and the economy. Men and women were given equal rights, factories were taken over by the government, and land was handed to the peasants.

However, agriculture was soon put under state control, and any extra grain was taken by the government to feed people in the towns. The economy began to collapse. The peasants held back grain, there were serious food shortages, and industrial production was reduced to less than a fifth of its level before World War I.

In the face of rising discontent, the Bolshevik leader Vladimir Lenin introduced the 'New Economic Policy'. This handed back small businesses to private owners and allowed peasant farmers to sell their own crops. By the time of Lenin's death in 1924 the economy had begun to get better.

A poster of Lenin. The caption at the bottom reads: 'The spectre that haunts Europe is Communism'.

The Great Depression

What Was the Great Depression?

The Great Depression was a period between 1929 and the mid-1930s during which many people were very poor because the world economy came near to collapse. Many banks and businesses closed down, resulting in high levels of unemployment and poverty in many countries of the world. The Great Depression only truly ended with the start of World War II at the end of the 1930s.

What Caused the Great Depression?

After its defeat in World War I, Germany was ordered to pay large amounts of money to Britain and France to compensate them for their losses. The USA, the richest and most powerful country in the world, had lent the European countries a lot of money to pay for the war, and these countries had to struggle to pay it back. The USA also began to export lots of goods to Europe, and soon they were producing more than was needed. At the same time people were investing a lot of money in the stock market, a system that allows people to buy and sell shares, or stocks, in businesses. If the business is successful the value of its shares rises.

By August 1929 share values had reached a peak, and were being bought at prices that were

way above the actual value of the companies. Then the share prices started to fall. Investors panicked and began selling their shares. The more shares were sold, the less they were worth. In October, as share prices got lower and lower, many people rushed to Wall Street, where the New York Stock Exchange was, only to discover that they had lost all their savings. Because of the panic about the falling prices of shares, everyone sold at once, causing the Wall Street Crash. It was this that started the Great Depression.

Life was very difficult for families caught up in the Great Depression.

Prohibition

In 1920, the US Congress passed the National Prohibition Act, which said it was illegal to brew or sell alcoholic drinks. Some people did not stop drinking or selling, however; they just did so illegally. This was the age of the gangster, the bootlegger (a person who sold 'bootleg', or alcohol), and the 'speakeasy' (an illegal bar).

Many people were in favour of Prohibition, but by the late 1920s they thought the government was wasting too much time and money on enforcing Prohibition laws and that they should have the freedom to choose whether or not to drink alcohol. With the start of the Great Depression, people argued that Prohibition took away jobs and money from the economy. Prohibition finally ended in 1933.

The Effects of the Great Depression

The Great Depression hit the USA first and hardest, but it quickly spread to Europe. People were poor and miserable. Many had to sell all their possessions, including their houses and cars, for very little money because they could not find work and needed money to buy food. Shanty towns sprang up in the USA and were called 'Hoovervilles' after Herbert Hoover who was the president during the Great Depression.

The New Deal

Franklin D Roosevelt promised the American people a 'new deal' if they would vote for him for president, and he won the 1932 election against Herbert Hoover by a landslide. In his inaugural speech he promised to fight against the Great Depression as if it were an enemy during war. His programme included money for farmers to help them produce food, construction programmes to create more jobs, and new laws to regulate banks and protect people's savings.

Al Capone (1899–1947)

Al Capone was one of the most famous and violent US gangsters of all time. He was known as 'Scarface' because of a scar from a knife cut on his left cheek. He was born in Naples, Italy, to Italian parents, but they moved to the USA when he was young, and he was brought up in Brooklyn, New York. He was not interested in school, left early, and spent the next ten years as a member of various gangs. In the 1920s he ran an organization in Chicago, Illinois, that made a lot of money by selling alcohol illegally. Over the years he got rid of his enemies and competitors, who were killed in gang wars, and gained control of Chicago's underworld (criminals). The police often ignored gang warfare, and so he was able to run his business uninterrupted for several years. He was finally imprisoned in 1931 for not paying his taxes.

Soup kitchens, where jobless people were given something to eat, appeared in cities in America during the Depression.

Social Reform and Suffrage: Britain 1901–1943

Social Changes

The early part of the 20th century saw a gradual improvement in the lives of working people in Britain. The Liberal government (1906–1911) introduced free school meals, old age pensions for people over 70, labour exchanges to help people find work, and national insurance for people who were ill or unemployed. The rich were taxed to pay for these reforms. The House of Lords tried to stop these new taxes, but the 1911 Parliament Act reduced the power of the House of Lords.

Workers from Jarrow in County Durham marched to London in 1936 after three quarters of the town's workers became unemployed.

In 1900 a committee of socialist groups was set up to promote a parliamentary party to represent working-class people. When 29 committee members were elected to parliament in 1906 they changed their name to the Labour Party.

Britain got its first Labour government in 1924, with Ramsay MacDonald becoming Britain's first Labour prime minister.

Trade Unions and Strikes

Trade unions, groups of workers in similar jobs, became stronger and were more able to negotiate the amount of money they earned and the hours they worked. Their strongest weapon was going on strike, refusing to work until their demands were met. There were many strikes between 1911 and 1914, especially in the railway, coalmining, and shipbuilding industries.

Work in Britain nearly came to a standstill in May 1926 when striking coal miners, protesting against pay cuts, asked other workers to join them in a general strike. Many did, but the effect of the strike was reduced by members of the public and the army doing the work of the strikers.

Economic Changes

On 24 October 1929 prices on Wall Street, the US Stock Exchange, fell sharply. Businesses failed and many people lost all their money. People all over the world lost their jobs. By 1932, 3 million people in Britain were unemployed.

In 1931 a National Government was formed in Britain, from all three political parties, to deal with the crisis. New industries grew up in the south and the Midlands bringing jobs and money. People could buy more and this helped create more jobs. But in the old industrial areas of coalmining, iron and steel, and shipbuilding there was still little work. People from these areas marched to London to try to force the government to help them. Help only came in the later 1930s, when the need to make guns, ships, and aircraft for World War II created new jobs.

Votes for Women

Only men could vote in general elections in 1901. Many people thought that women were not clever or responsible enough to vote. Women had been campaigning for the vote from the middle of the 19th century, and by 1900 the National Union of Women's Suffrage Societies (suffrage means the right to vote) was waging a peaceful campaign to persuade Parliament to bring in reforms. These campaigners were known as 'suffragists', but in 1903 a new, more radical organization was formed by Emmeline Pankhurst. This was the Women's Social and Political Union, whose members were called 'suffragettes'. The suffragettes drew attention to themselves by breaking windows, interrupting meetings, and chaining themselves to railings. They refused to pay their fines, got sent to prison, refused to eat, and were force-fed.

During World War I women earned much admiration for doing the work of men. After the war all men over the age of 21 and all women over the age of 30 were given the vote. Eventually, in 1928, all women over 21 were allowed to vote.

A Suffragette medal showing a photograph of Emmelline Pankhurst.

Suffragettes demonstrating at Westminster are expelled by the police.

Edward VIII (1894–1972) and Wallis Simpson (1896–1986)

Edward VIII became king on 21 January 1936 when his father, George V, died. He was 42, handsome and popular, but unmarried. He wanted to marry a twice-divorced American, Wallis Simpson. The prime minister, Stanley Baldwin, led the opposition to this marriage. No British newspaper reported the story so the British public knew nothing about it until the news broke in December 1936. Realizing that h s people would not accept Mrs Simpson as their queen, Edward decided to abdicate (give up the throne). On 11 December he made a farewell broadcast, ending with the words: 'God bless you all, God save the King'. His brother, George VI, was proclaimed king the next day.

Art, Architecture, and Design

Art Movements

The early 20th century saw a great explosion of experiments and new ideas and styles across literature, music, and art. Together, this movement is known as modernism. Modernist artists usually did not try to show objects or people realistically, and many of them painted completely abstract works (representing ideas rather than things), often using geometrical shapes.

The Sleep by Salvador Dali, one of the greatest of the Surrealist painters.

Marilyn, a portrait of Marilyn Monroe by Andy Warhol.

Expressionism was practised by many European artists, particularly in Germany, in the first three decades of the century. Expressionists believed in showing their emotions, rather than making perfect copies. Their work was intense, often including distorted faces and bodies, and with unrealistic colouring. Before World War I, Pablo Picasso and Georges Braque founded **Cubism**. They were concerned with the problems of showing solid objects on flat surfaces. Their work contains unexpected geometrical forms. These

forms, in fact, are part of the object portrayed, as seen from another angle. In the 1920s **Surrealists**, such as Salvador Dalí and René Magritte, became interested in new ideas about the importance of the mind. They painted strange dreamlike scenes, which, they felt, revealed hidden mysterious aspects of themselves and of all humans.

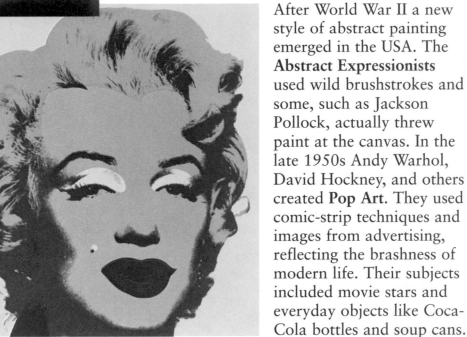

After World War II a new style of abstract painting emerged in the USA. The **Abstract Expressionists** used wild brushstrokes and some, such as Jackson Pollock, actually threw paint at the canvas. In the late 1950s Andy Warhol, David Hockney, and others created **Pop Art**. They used comic-strip techniques and images from advertising, reflecting the brashness of modern life. Their subjects included movie stars and everyday objects like Coca-Cola bottles and soup cans.

Pablo Picasso (1881–1973)

Pablo Picasso is considered the greatest 20th-century artist. He moved through many different styles of painting. He was an inventor of Cubism, and many of his best-known paintings, such as *Guernica* (1937), show Cubist influence. He produced brilliant drawings, and later in life he turned to sculpture and ceramics.

Architecture and Design

Art Deco

The Art Deco movement was named after a Paris exhibition, 'Modern Decorative and Industrial Arts', held in 1925. Buildings, furniture, ceramics, fashion, and jewellery were created in this rather playful style. It took elements from various styles, including Cubism and ancient Egyptian and Native American art.

Reaching for the Sky

The first skyscrapers were built in the USA at the end of the 19th century. In the first half of the 20th century the idea of building high was taken up by a number of modernist architects, including the Swiss architect Le Corbusier. His idea that houses should be 'machines for living in' resulted in huge concrete tower blocks. These have had an unfortunate influence on later, less skilful architects. The result is many of the bleak city buildings we see today. As well as concrete, other new building materials were also introduced in the 20th century. For example, the German architect Mies Van Der Rohe designed many beautiful skyscrapers made almost entirely of steel and glass.

Above, the Chrysler Building in New York built in 1930, with (left) one of the elevator doors inside, a fine example of the Art Deco style.

Henri Matisse (1869–1954)

Henri Matisse shocked the art world in 1905 with a style of painting involving bright, pleasing, non-realistic arrangements of colour and shape. He and his followers horrified critics, who called them **Fauves** ('wild beasts') because their work seemed so crude. Matisse's work changed, but throughout his life it remained colourful and joyful.

A Century of Books

Cheaper book production, the introduction of paperbacks, and more readers have meant a huge increase in the number of books published in the last hundred years.

Techniques in writing have changed. Novelists like E M Forster wrote in a traditional style, based around character and plot. James Joyce and Virginia Woolf experimented with techniques like 'stream of consciousness' (writing down the thoughts of the writer exactly as they occur).

Wars and Depression

The events of everyday life often affect themes in novels, plays, and poetry. During World War I, Rupert Brooke wrote patriotic poems while soldiers like Wilfred Owen and Siegfried Sassoon wrote about the horror and waste of war. In novels like *Sons and Lovers* (1913) D H Lawrence wrote about his theory that the modern world had a bad effect on human relationships.

From 1929 to the mid-1930s the world was in the middle of a depression, an economic crisis with high unemployment. John Steinbeck's novel *The Grapes of Wrath* (1939) described farming life in the USA during the depression. In contrast, F Scott Fitzgerald concentrated on the lifestyles of wealthy people who were unaffected by the country's economic problems.

Angry Young Men

In Britain in the 1950s and 1960s writers known as the 'Angry Young Men' wrote more realistically about ordinary people. The novel *Room at the Top* (1957), by John Braine, was one of the first to have a northern working-class man as the central character. Plays such as John Osborne's *Look Back in Anger* (1956) became known as 'kitchen-sink' drama, because their plots reflected the lives and emotions of ordinary people.

Women in Literature

The study of women in literature only became widespread from the late 1960s and 1970s. In 1973 the first women-only publisher, the Virago Press, was set up. Literature began to reflect more cultures and experiences, for example Maya Angelou's *I Know Why the Caged Bird Sings* (1970) and Alice Walker's *The Color Purple* (1982), both about the struggle of black women for freedom.

Children's Books

Since Beatrix Potter's *Peter Rabbit* (1902) animals have featured in 20th-century children's literature. These include 'real' creatures like those in Kenneth Grahame's *The Wind in the Willows* (1908); teddy-bears, like A A Milne's Winnie-the-Pooh; and friendly monsters like those in Maurice Sendak's *Where the Wild Things Are* (1963). The friends J R R Tolkein and C S Lewis wrote some of the most enduringly popular fantasy literature for children in *The Hobbit* (1937) and the Narnia tales (beginning with *The Lion, the Witch, and the Wardrobe* in 1950). More recently, Roald Dahl's appeal has been based on a combination of the fantastic and the grotesque. Authors who have written about children's everyday life and problems include Nina Bawden and Judy Blume.

Benjamin Bunny was one of many animal characters created by Beatrix Potter.

Comics

Billy Bunter, the fat hero of Greyfriars School, was born in 1908 with *The Magnet,* one of the first children's comics. *School Friend,* with Bessie Bunter, arrived for girls in 1919. The most outrageous characters, such as Desperate Dan and Dennis the Menace, came from the pages of *Dandy* in 1937 and *Beano* in 1938. The USA introduced the fantasy super hero with *Superman* in 1938 and *Batman* in 1939. Among the most famous comic-strip characters are Snoopy, Charles Schultz's daydreaming dog, and Asterix the Gaul, created by Albert Uderzo and René Goscinny.

The *Dandy* and the *Beano* have been popular with British children for over 60 years.

Fantasy and Science Fiction

Brave New World (1932) by Aldous Huxley and *Nineteen Eighty-Four* (1949) by George Orwell are early novels that imagine a frightening future. *The Lord of the Rings* (1954–1955), by J R R Tolkein, and the tales of Terry Pratchett are popular examples of fantasy writing. Reality and fantasy are combined in 'magic realism', a style used by Gabriel García Márquez in *One Hundred Years of Solitude* (1970) and Salman Rushdie in *Midnight's Children* (1981).

Martin Amis (left) and Salman Rushdie are two of the most influential writers of the late 20th century.

The Sound of Music

The variety and range of music created during the 20th century was astonishing. Sound recording made it possible for people to experience music of all kinds at the touch of a switch, and people listened to more music than ever before.

Debussy, Schoenberg, and Stravinsky

At the beginning of the 20th century Western musicians moved away from the emotional Romantic style and began to experiment. The French composer Claude Debussy created his own kinds of harmony, but the Austrian Arnold Schoenberg abandoned harmony and musical scales altogether. His music is very different, and some people find it hard to listen to.

The Russian Igor Stravinsky was one of the greatest composers of the century. His early ballet *The Rite of Spring* had a powerful, rhythmic style. Later he developed the Neoclassical style, in which he wrote modern pieces using the Classical style of the later 18th century as a starting point.

Tin Pan Alley and Jazz

In the early 20th century New York's Tin Pan Alley district was full of songwriters such as Cole Porter, Irving Berlin, and George Gershwin, writing songs that became very popular. Many of their songs were written for musicals, spectacular stage shows with singing and dancing.

In the southern USA, black musicians were developing new kinds of popular music. They mixed the African musical traditions of black slaves with American popular music. Blues was vocal music, in which the singer sang about the hardships of life. Jazz music had a swinging rhythm, and solo players improvised (made up variations) around the tune of the song.

Louis Armstrong, one of the greatest jazz trumpeters of the 20th century.

Rock and Pop

In the 1950s black Americans were playing a new style of blues called rhythm 'n' blues (R 'n' B). White musicians began to play their own version of R 'n' B, which became known as rock 'n' roll. Teenagers around the world danced to the music of the 1950s, and bought the records of stars like Elvis Presley, Buddy Holly, and Little Richard.

By the 1960s young musicians were creating new styles of rock music. Folk singer Bob Dylan added a rock beat to his songs of protest. In Britain the songs of John Lennon and Paul McCartney made the Beatles the most popular group in the world. Jimi Hendrix's high-energy electric guitar style became the basis of later heavy metal music. Soul singers combined rock rhythms with gospel-style singing.

Rock music continued to grow and change. In the 1970s Bob Marley made reggae music popular worldwide, and disco and funk were the hottest dance sounds. The harsh, violent sound of punk rock reacted against the way that the rock music industry focused on big money.

In the 1980s and 1990s new ways of making records produced a new range of sounds. Rap musicians improvised against a backing track, and DJs (disc jockeys) mixed and manipulated their records. Musicians playing house and techno music mixed sound 'samples' over a fast electronic beat. Electronic sounds dominated dance music, but bands such as Oasis were successful with a simple line-up of singer, guitars, and drums.

Opera

The greatest figure in opera in the early 20th century was the Italian composer Giacomo Puccini. Operas such as *La Bohème* and *Madame Butterfly* were immediate successes and are among the most popular operas in the world. Another popular writer of operas in a late Romantic style was the German composer Richard Strauss. Other composers such as Alban Berg began to experiment with more modern styles in their operas. Since World War II leading opera composers have included Benjamin Britten, whose first opera, *Peter Grimes,* was also a worldwide success. In his opera *Noye's Fludde,* which tells the story of Noah's Ark, most of the performers are children.

A spectacular modern staging of *Aida,* an opera by 19th-century composer Giuseppe Verdi.

Developments in Science

The early 20th century was a time of tremendous change in science. Basic ideas in physics were rethought, nuclear power was discovered, the mystery of inheritance (the question of why children are like their parents) was answered.

Common Sense Turned on its Head

In 1905 Albert Einstein completely changed our understanding of matter, space, and time when he published his special theory of relativity. Experimenters had discovered that the speed of light always seemed to be the same. It made no difference if the light source was moving away from or towards the observer. Einstein's theory set out to explain this by suggesting that the speed of light as it travels through space is always constant.

Strange Things at High Speeds

The speed of light is around 300,000 kilometres (186,000 miles) per second. Imagine you are on Earth and you flash a pulse of light to your friend zooming away in a spaceship at half the speed of light. Despite your friend's high speed, she will still measure the light passing her at 300,000 kilometres per second. Einstein showed that if the speed of light stays the same for both observers then time and space have to change. Speed, after all, is simply the time it takes to travel a distance. To you the clocks on your friend's ship appear to run slow. The light pulse can travel further in a given time because the time itself lasts longer! Einstein's theory therefore allows a type of time travel. Because time moves more slowly for the person in

Albert Einstein giving a lecture at Princetown University in the USA in 1931.

The Hidden Mind

At around the same time as physics was changing our view of the universe, the Austrian psychiatrist Sigmund Freud (1856–1939) was changing the way people think about the human mind. Until Freud's time, doctors had looked for physical changes in the brain to explain mental illnesses. Freud suggested that some types of mental illness arose in a deep part of the mind he called the unconscious. He found ways to treat these illnesses by talking to his patients about their childhood and their dreams. He learned things about their illnesses by asking them to 'free associate' – to say the first thing that came into their head when he said a word or phrase. Many people challenge Freud's ideas today.

the high-speed spaceship they would find when they returned to Earth that more time had passed for the people there. The space traveller would be in the future!

The Power of the Atom

In the 19th century atoms were thought to be the tiniest particles in the universe. But by the early 20th century physicists were discovering that atoms were made up of even tinier particles. The atom itself has a central nucleus made of protons and neutrons surrounded by a cloud of much lighter electrons.

In 1938 physicists in Germany found that a heavy uranium atom could be split into smaller, lighter pieces. This process was called fission, and it released huge amounts of energy. Within seven years this energy was used to make the first atomic reactor and the first atom bomb.

The Blueprint of Life

One of the great unsolved puzzles of biology in 1900 was how living things pass on their characteristics from parents to children. In the 1920s scientists studying fruit flies found that characteristics such as eye colour were passed on through structures inside cells called chromosomes. Chromosomes contained a chemical called DNA (deoxyribonucleic acid). But no one knew what DNA looked like, or how it worked.

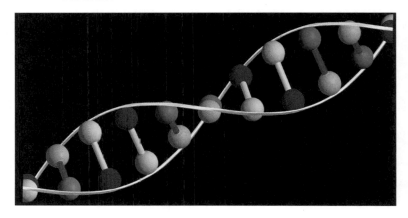

A simplified computer model of a short segment of the DNA molecule.

In 1953 Francis Crick and James Watson were able to show that DNA had a structure like a twisted ladder: two long chains of molecules twisted together, with 'rungs' of other molecules joining them. They learned that the DNA was a set of coded instructions to the cell for making a complete animal or plant.

Marie Curie (1867–1934) and Radioactivity

Marya Sklodowska was born in Poland in 1867. She studied chemistry at the Sorbonne (the University of Paris), where she met and married Pierre Curie. Together they studied the invisible rays given off by uranium. She called this phenomenon 'radioactivity'. Marie discovered two new elements, polonium and radium, both of which were many times more radioactive than uranium. As physicists understood more about the structure of atoms, it became clear that radioactivity came from the very heart of an atom – its nucleus. This was the starting point of nuclear physics. Marie was awarded two Nobel prizes and Pierre one for their work. She died in 1934 from the effects of radiation.

The Soviet Union under Stalin

Iosif Vissarionovich Dzugashvili (Stalin, meaning 'man of steel') was born in Georgia, a part of the old Russian empire. His father was a cobbler and his mother a washerwoman. He became a revolutionary and was arrested seven times between April 1902 and March 1913. He married in 1904 but his wife died three years later, leaving a son, Jacob.

Stalin rose to power after the Russian Revolution of 1917 and became dictator of the Soviet Union. Staying in power was more important to him than home life. He married his second wife in 1919 and she killed herself in 1932.

Stalin made the Soviet Union into a modern industrial nation and led it to victory in World War II. But millions of Soviet people died of poverty or were killed as Stalin's enemies. Stalin died suddenly in 1953. Some think he was murdered.

Joseph Stalin was absolute ruler of the Soviet Union for nearly 30 years.

Joseph Stalin became General Secretary of the Communist Party in 1922, even though he had done little in the 1917 Russian Revolution. After Lenin died in 1924, Stalin pushed out the Communists who had led the revolution. He took power for himself and by 1929 he had become the dictator of the Soviet Union.

Collectivization

In 1928 Stalin took control of the land from the middle-class farmers, the kulaks. Millions of them were sent into exile. The farms were collectivized, meaning they all came under state control. The grain harvest was seized from the peasants and sold abroad to pay for Stalin's programme of industrialization. This policy was obviously not popular. The peasants refused to work hard because most of their crops were taken by the government. Millions died from hunger and illness.

Ordinary people had to work long and hard to build Stalin's dream of a strong Russia.

Industrialization

Stalin's policy was to build 'socialism in one country'. This meant making the Soviet Union into a modern industrial country with powerful armed forces. In February 1931 he said: 'We are fifty or one hundred years behind the advanced countries ... We must make good the distance in ten years ... or we shall be crushed'.

Between 1928 and 1942 he developed three 'Five-Year Plans' to build up heavy industries such as coal, iron, steel, and machinery. Making goods that people needed in their daily lives was not important to Stalin. People in the factories had to work incredibly hard, even though in the seven years from 1929 the average wage was cut in half.

Purges

Stalin used his secret police to make sure that everyone did as they were told. From 1934 there were purges. Millions of people who Stalin thought might disagree with him were exiled (sent away) to freezing cold Siberia, forced to work in labour camps (where many died), or simply killed. No one knows exactly how many people died.

World War II

In 1941 Nazi Germany launched an invasion of the Soviet Union but failed to capture Moscow. The following year the German armies advanced to Stalingrad but the icy Russian winter and the stubborn resistance of the Russian people resulted in a major defeat. The Germans were forced to retreat pursued by the Soviet Red Army, which swept the Germans back across Eastern Europe. The Red Army captured the German capital, Berlin, in May 1945. The Soviet Union – especially the western part – suffered terribly in the war. In all, around 27 million Soviet soldiers and civilians died. After the war the USSR gained a huge empire in Eastern Europe. Stalin took over the governments of several countries and made them Communist. This led to conflict with the West called the Cold War.

Leon Trotsky, one of the leaders of the Russian Revolution, hated Stalin.

Leon Trotsky (1879–1940)

Lev Davidovich Bronstein (Trotsky) was a Jewish Russian who became a revolutionary in 1896. Between 1898 and 1917 he was arrested and exiled to Siberia twice, both times escaping and going abroad. Trotsky played a leading role in the Russian Revolution, and led the Red Army to victory during the civil war that followed.

After Lenin's death, Trotsky opposed Stalin's rise to power. Trotsky believed that the Russian Revolution had to spread to the rest of the world to be successful. Stalin disagreed, and forced Trotsky out of the Communist Party. In 1927 Trotsky called Stalin the 'gravedigger of the revolution'. Trotsky was sent into exile and lived in a number of countries before he reached Mexico in 1936. One of Stalin's agents killed him with an ice pick in 1940.

Nazi Germany

How Hitler Came to Power

The Weimar Republic, Germany's government from 1919 to 1933, was neither strong nor popular. It was blamed for everything that went wrong – defeat in World War I, unemployment, poverty, and inflation. Adolf Hitler became very popular when he claimed that Germany had not lost the war but had been betrayed, 'stabbed in the back', by socialists. He promised the German people that he would rebuild the army and unite with Austria. He told them that their problems were all caused by Jews and communists.

Faced with no jobs, no food, and no money – largely as a result of the world economic depression – the German people wanted to believe that Hitler and his Nazi Party could help them. In the 1932 elections for the German Reichstag (parliament), the Nazis won the most seats, although they did not win a majority. In January 1933 Adolf Hitler was appointed chancellor (prime minister) of Germany.

Did You Know?

The swastika, a cross with the ends bent over at right angles, is a very ancient symbol. It represents the daily journey of the sun and is a symbol of rebirth and prosperity. For the Nazis the swastika represented the way Germany would be reborn and prosper under their rule.

Adolf Hitler, who declared himself Führer, or absolute leader, of Germany in 1934.

The Nazis staged huge triumphal gatherings such as this one to display their strength.

Once in power, Hitler made himself into a dictator. He abolished parliamentary government and banned other political parties. People who did not like this were arrested, imprisoned, tortured, and put to death – all without trial. In 1935 the rights of German citizenship were removed from all Jews.

The Nazis' vicious behaviour was made all the worse by the fact that they were such efficient organizers. Soon every aspect of German life was taken over by some part of the Nazi organization. The police, law, trade unions, the church, youth movements, and women's organizations were all controlled by the Nazis. Many people liked the Nazi Party, and became members, because it reduced unemployment and promised to make Germany strong again. Even for those people who did not like the Nazis, it was wise not to become their enemy.

The Final Solution

To the Nazis the Jews were the source of all the evils of society. The Nazis determined to remove them from German life. Jews – anyone with even a single Jewish grandparent – had their jobs and businesses taken away from them and were refused service in shops, hotels, and restaurants. Hooligans who beat them up went unpunished. Throughout the 1930s thousands of Jews left Germany.

The Nazis were happy with this solution, but when war broke out the Nazis prevented the Jews from emigrating. They intended to exterminate the Jews. At first the Jews were rounded up and shot, but this was not efficient enough for the Nazis so another solution had to be found. The Jews were sent to concentration camps, and these were turned into death factories. Here Jews were herded into gas chambers, 2,000 at a time, and killed. The gold from their teeth, the hair from their heads, and the fat from their flesh was then used in the German war effort.

In this terrible way over 6 million Jews were killed in what the Nazis called 'the final solution'. This mass murder of the Jews of Europe is now known as 'the Holocaust'.

Anne Frank (1929–1945)

Anne Frank was a German Jewish girl forced to live in hiding with her family for two years in the German-occupied Netherlands. During these two years Anne kept a diary, an accurate record of their daily life under extraordinary circumstances. One day they were betrayed to the Gestapo, the Nazi secret police, and taken to a concentration camp, Belsen, where Anne died. Her father survived. After the war he published her diary. The story of one Jewish girl amongst the 6 million killed touched people's hearts all over the world.

Anne Frank, just one of the many victims of the Nazi reign of terror.

Pages from Anne Frank's diary, telling of her life in hiding from the Nazis.

The Rise of Fascism: Italy and Spain

Mussolini and Fascism

On 23 March 1919 Benito Mussolini, an Italian ex-soldier, formed the Fasci di Combattimento. The name was meant to suggest a group of fighters bound together as tightly as the rods and axes of the fascine, the symbol of the power and authority of ancient Rome. The members wore black shirts, and became known as 'fascists'. They were an elite group who glorified war and fighting and used violence to get their own way. They did not believe in parliaments, elections, or any form of democracy, but, unlike communists, they were not against religion, wealth, or property.

In 1936 Italy and Germany formed an alliance called the Axis.

Mussolini watches a march past of women fascists in 1939.

W HITLER   W MVSSOLINI

The Rise of Mussolini

After World War I the Italians were angry that Yugoslavia had been given land on the Adriatic Sea that they had always wanted. Inside Italy work was hard to find, wages were low, and there was much poverty and hardship. Under these conditions communist ideas spread. The activities of the communists provoked fierce street fights with fascists. Fascism was more popular with Italians than communism because it did not threaten the middle and upper classes. In 1922 the communists called a general strike. Mussolini said that he and his Blackshirts would crush the strike if the government was too feeble to act, and led his supporters in a march on Rome. The king of Italy, Victor Emmanuel III, admired Mussolini's power and popularity and invited him to become prime minister.

Soldiers of the Republican army during the Spanish Civil War.

The Spanish Civil War

Elections in February 1936 voted in a left-wing government in Spain that was sympathetic to the communists. In July the army rebelled, fearing a communist takeover. By the end of July, Spain was divided. The rebels, known as the Nationalists, mostly held the north, and the government forces, known as the Republicans, held the south, although the civil war divided towns, villages, and even families.

Amongst the Nationalist supporters were Falangists, Spanish fascists, so General Franco, the nationalist leader, appealed to the fascist governments of Germany and Italy for help. The Republicans appealed to Britain and France. Britain, fearing that the situation in Spain might lead to another world war, tried to persuade other countries to agree not to send help. Germany and Italy agreed, but had no intention of keeping their word. German and Italian forces were sent to help the Nationalists, and tested their new planes, tanks, and guns against the Republicans. The Republicans eventually got some help from communist Russia and from the International Brigade, armies of mostly communist volunteers.

By Christmas 1936 Spain had become the battleground for a European struggle between communists and fascists. The foreign reinforcements prolonged what was already a bloody and bitter struggle. In March 1939 Madrid surrendered to the Nationalists who were ultimately better armed, better trained, and better disciplined than the Republicans. The war was over, and Franco, with the support of the falangists, was to rule Spain as a virtual dictator until his death in 1975.

Did You Know?

The phrase 'fifth columnists', meaning enemies inside your own camp, came from the Spanish Civil War. In October 1936 Nationalist troops were advancing on Madrid, which was held by the Republicans. General Mola, commander of the Nationalists, said that he had four army columns marching on Madrid and that there was a fifth column inside the city made up of those who would support him when the time came.

Italians were encouraged to see their new prime minister as a hero, and Mussolini himself took the title of *Duce* (leader). His popularity grew as his government built schools, roads, railways, bridges, and hospitals. However, the fascist government was involved in the murder of the socialist leader Giacomo Matteotti in 1924, and after this Mussolini became a dictator, imprisoning opponents, controlling what the newspapers reported, and bullying workers. In 1935 Mussolini invaded and conquered Abyssinia (Ethiopia). Italians were thrilled, but this was the peak of Mussolini's popularity. He got involved in more foreign ventures, like the Spanish Civil War, which Italy could not afford. These drew Italy into closer contact with Germany, where the Nazis (German fascists) were in power under Adolf Hitler. Together the two countries took the disastrous road to war.

World War II in the West

World War II started in Europe, but soon turned into a global war. The war was fought between the Axis powers (principally Germany, Italy, and Japan) and the Allied powers (principally Britain, the Commonwealth, France, the USA, the USSR, and China).

extent of the Axis Powers by November 1942

Allied Powers

neutral state

that a strong Germany would act as a barrier against the communist Soviet Union (USSR). This policy became known as 'appeasement'. Hitler was allowed to build up Germany's armed forces, and Britain and France stood by when Hitler took over Austria in March 1938 and then Czechoslovakia in March 1939. Hitler now demanded the return of territory from Poland. On 23 August Hitler signed a non-aggression pact with his sworn enemy the Soviet Union, which gave him access to Poland. But Britain and France were ready to stop further Nazi aggression, and when Germany invaded Poland on 1 September, they declared war.

The Course of the War

In the spring of 1940 Germany invaded and conquered Denmark, Norway, France, Belgium, the Netherlands, and Luxembourg. The British army only just managed to escape from France at Dunkirk. As France fell, Italy joined the German side. By this time Winston Churchill had become prime minister in Britain, and refused German offers of peace. Hitler now made plans to invade Britain, but his attempt to destroy the British air force was defeated in the Battle of Britain (August and September). The German air force began instead to bomb British cities ('the Blitz'), while German submarines in the Atlantic tried to stop the delivery of essential supplies from the USA to Britain.

The Road to War

Germany had been defeated in World War I, and in 1919 was forced to accept the Treaty of Versailles. The treaty blamed Germany for starting the war, made it give up large areas of territory, greatly reduced its armed forces, and demanded the payment of huge amounts of money. During the worldwide economic depression of the 1930s, unemployment in Germany was high. Adolf Hitler, leader of the Nazi Party, rose to power in 1933. He was popular for his theory that the Treaty of Versailles was responsible for Germany's current troubles and that the only answer was to overthrow the treaty.

At first, when Hitler disobeyed the treaty, Britain and France did nothing, believing that the treaty had treated Germany harshly and hoping

In the meantime, the war spread. In North Africa fierce fighting raged for nearly three years. In the spring of 1941 Hitler occupied the Balkans. Britain fought alone until June 1941, when Hitler invaded the Soviet Union, and the Japanese attack on Pearl Harbor brought the USA into the war in December. The British victory at El Alamein in Egypt in 1942 and the

30

Soviet victory at Stalingrad in 1942–1943 turned the tide of the European war. Allied troops landed in Sicily in July 1943, and Italy changed sides. However, German forces moved into Italy and fighting continued. On D-Day, 6 June 1944, Allied troops landed in Normandy, France, and pushed towards Germany. Meanwhile, the Soviet Red Army was advancing through Eastern Europe. Soviet troops reached the German capital, Berlin, in April 1945. Hitler committed suicide, and Germany surrendered on 8 May.

The British Expeditionary Force escapes from Dunkirk in 1940.

The Home Front

No cheering crowds greeted the outbreak of war in 1939 as they had done in 1914. This time, however, Britain was better prepared. Rearmament (supplying the army with better weapons) had been in progress since 1938, and limited conscription (required military service) was introduced in April 1939. Air attacks were the greatest fear, so gas masks were provided for civilians and air-raid shelters were dug. Over a million mothers and children were evacuated from the cities, out of reach of expected bombing raids. The blackout meant no building or vehicle was allowed to show a light at night. When the German bombers came they brought death and devastation. On one night, 10 May 1941, 1,400 Londoners were killed and many buildings were destroyed including the House of Commons.

Everyone had to help the war effort. Women joined the Land Army to grow food, worked in factories, and drove trains and buses. After December 1941 they were called up for military service. Food, fuel, clothes, and furniture were rationed so that maximum effort could be put into producing weapons.

In 1940 more than 120,000 children were evacuated from London to safer counties in the south west of England.

World War II in the Far East and Pacific

Japanese Expansion

Although Japan was a fast growing industrial nation, it was a small country and it wanted more land and oil. In the 1930s its government was increasingly dominated by the military. In 1931 the Japanese seized Manchuria, and in 1937 they attacked China. The European war, which began in 1939, left only the USA to stand in the way of Japan's expansion. Japan and the USA were not at war when, on the morning of 7 December 1941, the Japanese launched a surprise attack on the American Pacific Fleet anchored in Pearl Harbor, Hawaii. The USA was outraged and declared war.

Over the next five months the Japanese were triumphant. By May 1942 Hong Kong, Singapore, Malaya, Burma, Thailand, French Indochina (now Vietnam, Cambodia, and Laos), the Philippines, the Dutch East Indies (now Indonesia), Borneo, New Guinea, and many islands in the Pacific Ocean were all in Japanese hands. The Japanese had even bombed Darwin in northern Australia.

US Marines raise the flag on top of Mount Kiribachi after their successful assault on the Pacific island of Iwo Jima.

Kamikaze

To the samurai, an ancient order of Japanese knights, death was preferable to either surrender or defeat. In 1945, as the US Navy closed in on the Japanese mainland, it became vital for the Japanese to destroy US ships. Torpedoes, shells, and bombs could miss, so Japanese pilots volunteered to fly their bomb-laden planes straight into ships. This was suicide for the Japanese pilot, but as a result 34 US ships were sunk and 5,000 lives lost. These kamikaze pilots were named after a typhoon that destroyed a Mongol fleet threatening Japan in 1281. The name means 'divine wind'.

Operation Centreboard

On 6 August 1945, a single atomic bomb, dropped from the American B-29 bomber *Enola Gay,* was detonated 560 metres (1,850 feet) above the Japanese city of Hiroshima and exploded with the equivalent force of 20,000 tons of TNT. In an instant more than 80,000 people were killed. A fireball engulfed the city, followed by an 800 kilometres (500 miles) per hour wind. A large area of Hiroshima was reduced to charred rubble. In total, more than 88,000 people were killed by the explosion. Many thousands more died as a result of radioactive dust falling over the Japanese countryside, poisoning people, animals, and the land for years to come. The first atomic bomb had been tested only 21 days earlier, over the wide open wastes of the desert in New Mexico.

Part of the devastation caused to the US Pacific fleet after the Japanese attack at Pearl Harbor in 1941.

The Tide Turns

On 4 June 1942 the US and Japanese navies met off Midway Island, an important US base in the middle of the Pacific Ocean. During a five-minute dive-bomb attack the Americans sank three Japanese aircraft carriers and destroyed over 300 aeroplanes. This was the turning point of the war. Although it took the USA and British Commonwealth three more years to defeat Japan, in the end their naval and air superiority won the day.

Slowly the Japanese were driven back through the jungles of Burma and through hundreds of tiny Pacific islands. The Japanese resisted every inch of the way. In June 1945 US forces took the islands of Okinawa and Iwo Jima, only 640 kilometres (400 miles) from the Japanese mainland. Japan was defeated but would not surrender. On 6 August an atomic bomb was dropped on the Japanese city of Hiroshima. Three days later a second bomb was dropped on Nagasaki. Over 140,000 Japanese citizens were killed by these explosions, and many more were killed by the after effects. Six days later the emperor of Japan announced to his people that the war was over.

A mushroom cloud rises above the Japanese city of Nagasaki after the detonation of an atomic bomb on 9 August 1945.

Peacemaking after World War II

After World War II the Allies divided Germany into four occupation zones. Austria became independent of Germany and was also occupied by the Allies. The Soviet Red Army occupied Eastern Europe, and by 1948 all Eastern European countries had communist governments. It was said that an 'Iron Curtain' had fallen across Europe, dividing the communist from the noncommunist countries.

Allied leaders Winston Churchill, Franklin Roosevelt, and Joseph Stalin meet at Yalta in 1945 near the end of the war.

Happy people in London celebrate the end of the war in Europe.

The Threat of Communism

Russia was once an ally of Britain and the USA but it became an enemy because of its communist government. Under a plan known as the Truman Doctrine, in 1947 the USA promised money and materials to old enemies and allies if they resisted communism. The Marshall Plan, begun in 1948, provided further help to Western European countries – food, fuel, machinery, and raw materials – partly also as a reward for resisting communism. In 1949 the North Atlantic Treaty Organization (NATO) was created. Its members, including the USA, Canada, and 10 countries in Western Europe, made a pact to fight the spread of communism.

The Nuremberg Trials

Twenty-two of Germany's Nazi leaders were tried at Nuremberg, in Germany, for crimes they had committed during the war. These crimes included the cold-blooded murder of about 16 million people in concentration camps, including about 6 million Jews. The trials opened on 20 November 1945 and lasted 218 days. The world was shocked as it heard for the first time of some of the atrocities (cruel and wicked acts) that had been committed. Eventually, 12 of the 22 were sentenced to death. The executions were fixed for 16 October 1946. A few hours before the appointed time Hermann Goering, one of the most infamous of the surviving Nazis, committed suicide.

The Nurmeberg Trials lasted for nearly a year, from November 1945 to October 1946.

Other main Nazi leaders, including Joseph Goebbels and Adolf Hitler himself, committed suicide before the trials started and so were never tried for their crimes.

A Community in Europe

A growing desire rose among the countries of Western Europe to link together to make another war unthinkable. In 1957 the Treaty of Rome created the European Economic Community (EEC), which established free trade between the member countries. The original members were France, Belgium, Luxembourg, the Netherlands, Italy, and West Germany. In 1973 the United Kingdom, Ireland, and Denmark joined. The organization changed its name to the European Community (EC), and in 1993 it became the basis of the European Union (EU). By the end of the century people in member countries were free to move across borders in Europe, and they developed a common legal and monetary system. A single European currency, the euro, was first introduced in 1999.

The United Nations

To avoid war and help maintain peace, the United Nations (UN) was created in 1945. Membership is open to all countries. Members send representatives to the General Assembly, a kind of world parliament. A Security Council, made up of 11 member states, meets more regularly to try and reduce tension before it leads to war. Members are expected to provide troops, when necessary, to police trouble spots. Recognizing that the huge divide between rich and poor nations could be a source of future trouble, the UN has created specialized agencies to help educate, feed, and provide medical care for the people of the world.

Transport on Land and Sea

At the start of the 20th century trains were the best way to get about on land, while ships were the only way to cross the seas. By the end of the century road transport was more important than rail, and airliners had replaced the luxury ocean liners.

Atlantic Crossings

In the late 19th century ocean liners competed for the 'Blue Ribbon', given for the fastest crossing of the Atlantic Ocean. In the early 20th century faster, more powerful steam-turbine engines were introduced, and liners became enormous. The largest ship of the time was the *Titanic*, built in 1912. It was thought to be unsinkable, but on its first voyage it hit an iceberg and sank, and more than 1,500 people died.

In the 1920s and 1930s the Atlantic liners reached their peak of luxury, speed, and size. The French ship *Normandie* had room for nearly 2,000 passengers and a crew of over 1,300. In 1952 the SS *United States* made the fastest-ever Atlantic crossing, completing the voyage in just under three and a half days. However, this was slow compared to the few

This poster gives an impression of how stylish it was to travel on a large ocean liner.

France's superfast TGV train speeds through the French countryside.

The End of the Steam Train

As more people used cars, fewer used trains. In the early 1900s railways still relied on steam power. But in the 1920s and 1930s many countries began to use electric and diesel trains, which were cleaner than steam trains and used less fuel. By the 1960s they had replaced steam trains almost completely.

As cars got faster, trains speeded up, too. In 1964 a new high-speed train line was opened in Japan, between Tokyo and Osaka. The Shinkansen or 'bullet train' travelled at speeds of up to 240 kilometres (150 miles) per hour. An even faster train began running in France in the 1980s – the TGV (Train à Grand Vitesse or 'high-speed train'). It had a maximum speed of 300 kilometres (180 miles) per hour. Today many European countries run TGV trains.

A Model T Ford production line in one of Henry Ford's factories. Making cars like this meant they could be produced cheaply and in great numbers.

hours taken by the jet airliners that began to fly the Atlantic in the 1950s. The age of the huge ocean liners had passed.

Cars in their Millions

In 1900 cars were rich people's toys, hand-built and very expensive. But by the 1920s they were being made cheaply and in their millions. This change was largely due to one man – the US industrialist Henry Ford. Henry Ford built his first car in 1896. He wanted to build a 'car for the people' that was cheap to buy and easy to run. In 1907 he reorganized his factory into 'assembly lines', where each person put together only one part of each car. This way, cars could be made much faster and more cheaply. The Model T Ford was the first car built this way when production started in 1908. It was an enormous success: over 16 million were made before production stopped in 1927.

Soon other manufacturers were also producing cars in huge numbers. As the numbers of cars grew, the numbers of roads grew too. By 1915 there were more roads than railways. The first motorways were built in Italy in the 1920s.

By the end of the century, however, many people were concerned about the damage new roads can do to the environment, and about the effect of the exhaust fumes of so many cars on people's health.

Traffic Safety

Traffic lights were first used in New York in 1915. They were introduced for safety and to help keep traffic moving. Another safety device, the cat's eye, was invented in the UK in 1934. Cat's eyes help drivers at night by showing up the centre and edges of the road.

Record Tunnels

The world's two longest tunnels were built as part of high-speed railway lines. The Japanese Seikan Tunnel, which links the main island of Honshu with the smaller northern island of Hokkaido, is the longest tunnel in the world – nearly 54 kilometres (34 miles) from end to end. In Europe the 50-kilometre (31-mile) Channel Tunnel runs under the English Channel between England and France.

Transport in the Air

By 1900 people had flown in balloons and in gliders. But neither balloons nor gliders had engines. True powered flight had yet to be achieved.

The Wright Flyer

In the 1890s Wilbur and Orville Wright, two US bicycle-makers from Dayton, Ohio, became interested in flight. They began building gliders, testing them in the hills of North Carolina. In 1903 they put an engine in their latest glider and in December of that year Orville Wright made the first true aeroplane flight. In 1907 the Wright brothers set out to build a 2-man aeroplane for the US Army Signal Corps. It was delivered in 1909, the year that Louis Bleriot made the first flight across the English Channel in a small aircraft.

The Wright brother's Flyer, the first heavier-than-air powered flying machine, which flew on 17 December 1903.

Helicopters

The idea of a helicopter was a dream for hundreds of years before the first flight took place. The great Italian artist and inventor Leonardo da Vinci sketched a helicopter design in his notebooks in the 15th century.

In the early 20th century primitive models made very short flights, but then in 1923 the Spaniard Juan de la Cierva built a successful autogyro. This was an aeroplane with rotors that were not powered, but which gave the plane lift when it was moved forwards by a propeller. In 1936 German engineers developed the first practical helicopter, the Focke-Angelis Fa 61. This flew to a height of 3,500 metres (11,500 feet), and a distance of over 230 kilometres (140 miles).

Airlines and Records

During World War I (1914–1918) aircraft became more reliable, more powerful, and more agile. Planes with two, three, or four engines were built to carry bombs. After the war, the first airlines began operating. The early airliners could travel only a few hundred kilometres between stops, but by the 1930s four-engined flying boats were being used for flights half-way across the world.

In this period there were many flying firsts. John Alcock and Arthur Brown made the first non-stop flight across the Atlantic Ocean from Newfoundland to Ireland in 1919 in a Vickers Vimy. Then in 1927 the American Charles Lindbergh, who had been a stunt flier, made the first non-stop solo flight from New York to Paris.

Jet Power

In 1939 World War II began. Aircraft developed quickly as each side tried to build faster fighters and better-armed bombers. But the greatest development of the time was the jet engine.

The British engineer Frank Whittle first had the idea for a jet-powered plane in 1927. By 1937 he had built a full-sized engine. But in the 1930s the German engineers Otto Pabst and Hans von Ohain also began developing jets. Ernst Heinkel built two planes, one of which, the Heinkel HE 178, made the first jet flight in 1939. After World War II people began to discover the real potential of the jet engine, as jet aircraft smashed speed records set by propeller-driven planes. Within a short time military jets were flying faster than the speed of sound.

The first commercial jet airliner was the De Havilland Comet, which started to fly passengers in 1952. This was followed by bigger airliners such as the Boeing 707, which entered service in 1958. Most jet airliners travel at less than the speed of sound, because supersonic planes use much more fuel. But in 1974 the Concorde, built jointly in Britain and France, became the first supersonic airliner to begin regular flights.

Amelia Earhart (1897–1937)

In the 1920s women were also learning to fly. A year after Charles Lindbergh crossed the Atlantic, Amelia Earhart became the first woman to make the trip by plane. On this flight she was simply the navigator, but four years later, in 1932, she piloted her own plane and became the first woman to fly solo across the Atlantic.

In 1937, while attempting a round-the-world flight, Amelia's plane disappeared over the Pacific Ocean. Despite many weeks of searching, it was never found.

Airport Technology

Busy airports today handle thousands of passengers and hundreds of flights each day. Air traffic controllers, working from the airport's control tower, tell pilots when it is safe to take off or land. They use radar to track aircraft as they come into and out of the airspace around the airport. At night and in poor weather aircraft are guided onto the runway using signals from a radar beam on the ground.

Medical Advances throughout the Century

Medicine has developed enormously in the 20th century. It has helped people to live longer, healthier lives. But some types of illness have proved hard to cure, and outbreaks of previously unknown diseases are a cause for concern.

Fighting Disease

By the end of the 19th century scientists knew about the bacteria and other microbes that cause diseases. In the 1930s the first drugs effective against bacteria were discovered: the sulphonamides used for blood infections, and penicillin, the first antibiotic, which cured a whole range of infections. From the 1950s onwards hundreds of new drugs were discovered. Many were extracted from plants and bacteria, but soon chemists were able to make drugs artificially.

Improvements in health care such as inoculation benefit people around the world.

Another successful method of preventing disease was to use vaccines, which make the person's body develop defences against disease. The method was first introduced in the 18th century by Edward Jenner against smallpox, but in the 20th century vaccines were developed for many more diseases, such as tetanus, diphtheria, and polio.

Surgery

By the 20th century anaesthetics (drugs used to make people unconscious) had taken the pain from surgery and the use of antiseptics had reduced the risk of infection, but there were still many deaths. From the 1920s blood transfusions helped prevent deaths caused by blood loss.

Many types of surgery developed as surgeons learned new skills and new technologies were invented. It became possible to replace

An anaesthetic device developed for use by the military in the 1950s. It would have been used for battlefield surgery.

Cancers

Cancers are still a major cause of death around the world. These are diseases in which a group of body cells begins to grow in an abnormal way. Chemotherapy (using chemicals to treat disease) is sometimes able to cure cancers, often in combination with surgery to remove the cancerous cells. The causes of some cancers are not known, although smoking is known to increase the chances of lung cancer.

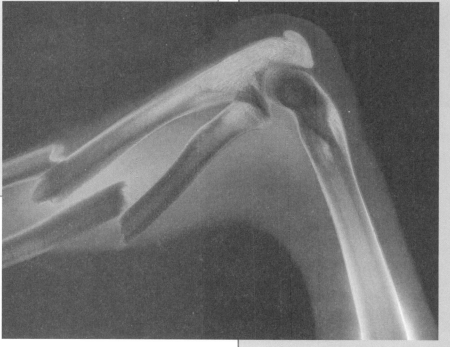

An X-ray image of a broken arm.

damaged or worn-out tissues, for example using plastic heart valves or metal hip joints. The heart-lung machine helped heart surgeons by taking over the patient's circulation and breathing while the surgeon worked on the heart.

The first heart transplant was performed in 1967. As with other transplants, the main challenge was to stop the patient's body rejecting the new organ. Drugs that stopped the body's natural immune defences from rejecting the new organ as a 'foreign body' helped make transplants more successful.

Since the 1980s, microsurgery, using a powerful operating microscope, has been very successful for eye, ear, and brain operations. Lasers are also used for very accurate work. Some operations have been made safer through keyhole surgery, where the surgeon operates using fibre-optic tubes inserted through a small cut.

Looking inside the Body

Diagnosis and treatment of illness has been greatly helped by machines that let the doctor look inside the body without opening it up. X-rays were discovered in 1895, and were quickly developed to enable doctors to look at bones. In the early 20th century machines that looked at electrical activity in the heart were introduced, and in the 1920s a similar machine detected activity in the brain. In the 1970s it became possible to scan cross-sections of the body using X-rays, then use computers to build up a complete 3D picture of the body. Other kinds of scanner were also developed, such as ultrasound scanners, which can be used where X-rays would be harmful, for example, to look at babies in the womb. Magnetic resonance imaging (MRI) is another new technique. MRI scanners can give detailed information about the brain and central nervous system.

New Health Risks

In recent years the appearance of completely new diseases has caused health worries. The viral disease AIDS, which causes the body's immune system to break down, was discovered in 1981. Ebola, which causes fever and often death, is a new viral disease in Africa. Bacteria resistant to nearly all known drugs are causing problems in some hospitals. There are large gaps in our knowledge about these new health risks. But in all cases simple precautions such as careful hygiene can make the risks of such illnesses very small.

Cinema and Television

Stephen Spielberg (1947–)

Stephen Spielberg is a modern master of cinematic effects. *Jaws* (1975), starring a great white shark, was his first smash hit. He used impressive special effects for films about other creatures, an alien in *E.T.* (1982), and dinosaurs in *Jurassic Park* (1993). He also produced some serious and critically acclaimed adult films, such as *Schindler's List* (1993), a movie about the suffering of Jews in Hitler's death camps, and *Saving Private Ryan* (1998), a movie set during World War II showing the horrors of war.

Sir Richard Attenborough on the set of *Jurassic Park*.

The Development of the Cinema

The first cinema shows were held in 1895. The films were very simple, in black and white, silent, and short. Technical development was rapid, and the 1913 film *Quo Vadis* was two hours long. Sound was introduced in 1927, and the 'talkies' took off. In the 1930s techniques for adding colour were developed, the best known being Technicolor. The techniques were complicated, and colour was not used widely until the 1950s. The 1950s also saw the development of wide-screen presentation. Most cinemas now use this system.

The Development of Television

In 1926 the Scottish electrical engineer John Logie Baird demonstrated the first television set, in London. In 1928 colour TV was demonstrated at the Bell Laboratories in the USA. Also in 1928 the BBC broadcast the first TV programme, and in 1929 adopted Baird's system. The same year saw the first regular US TV broadcasts. However, Baird's system used mechanical as well as electronic components, and was rather cumbersome. In the 1930s TV companies adopted an all-electronic system, using a cathode-ray tube in the receiver, based on the inventions of the Russian-born US physicist Vladimir Zworykin. It was with this system that the BBC launched its first public TV broadcast service from Alexandra Palace in

North London in 1936. In the 1950s US TV began colour broadcasts. The coronation of Queen Elizabeth II, in 1953, was televised worldwide. The Eurovision TV network was opened in 1954, and in 1962 the satellite Telstar transmitted live TV from the USA to Europe. Today, television broadcasts reach people's homes by a variety of routes: from transmitters on the ground, from satellite transmitters, or through electrical cables.

The puppets Pinky and Perky were popular stars of early children's television.

Charles Chaplin's much-loved silent films made him one of the world's best-known faces in the 1920s.

The Star System

Cinema gives us the illusion of being really close to the people we see on film. We see tiny changes of expression, and seem to know what they are thinking and feeling. Films reach many people, in many countries. Early in the history of cinema, film actors became enormously famous and hugely popular. When the glamorous Rudolph Valentino died aged 31 in 1926, fans all over the Western world were hysterical. Among the great stars are:

- Charlie Chaplin, the great clown of silent movies;
- Marlene Dietrich, a glamorous German with a deep, sexy voice;
- Clark Gable, idolized by millions of women;
- Marilyn Monroe, the sex symbol of the 20th century, whose childlike appeal endeared her to women as well as men;
- James Dean, the symbol of teenage rebellion, killed in a car crash in 1955, aged 24;
- English-born Elizabeth Taylor, a star since her childhood, whose beauty and fighting spirit has survived eight marriages and many bouts of serious illness;
- John Wayne, the all-American cowboy hero;
- Sylvester (Sly) Stallone, whose portrayal of 'tough guys' set new standards in US cinema;
- Leonardo di Caprio, whose blue-eyed boyish good looks have touched the hearts of many young women today.

Directors

Film directors decide what character and style a film should have. The history of cinema is the story of some great directors. The Soviet director Sergei Eisenstein was hugely influential. He explored the use of powerful crowd scenes, and was best-known for the way he put images together to produce emotional effects. *The Battleship Potemkin* (1925) is his best-known film. The English director Alfred Hitchcock was a master of horror and suspense. His effects came not from the liberal use of horrifying images, but from the slow, sure build-up of fear. His well-known films include *Rear Window* (1954), *Psycho* (1960), and *The Birds* (1963).

India: The Jewel in Britain's Crown

The British Raj

After the Indian Mutiny of 1857–1858 Britain took over the government of India from the British East India Company. The British government of India became known as the Raj (Raj is an Indian word for rule). India was seen as the finest of Britain's colonies. The British built thousands of miles of railways in India, and also introduced Western-style education. But they also ran the economy of India for the benefit of industrialists back in Britain, and for most of India's poor peasants life did not improve.

The Indian National Congress

In 1885 the Indian National Congress ('Congress' for short) was formed by a few educated Indians who disliked British rule and who believed that India should be run by Indians. More and more people joined Congress and by 1910 most of them no longer wanted to

Cowpat boys in India. The cowpats are burned for fuel.

deal with the British. They wanted to be independent and form their own government.

The Amritsar Massacre

On 13 April 1919, 5,000 ordinary Indians gathered peacefully in a park in Amritsar to listen to the nationalists talking about independence. British army commander General Dyer panicked at seeing so many people, and told his soldiers to open fire. In 15 minutes 379 people were dead and some 1,200 injured. After this massacre many Indians became even more determined to fight for independence.

Gandhi and Satyagraha

The most famous campaigner for independence was Mahatma Gandhi. Along with Jawaharlal Nehru – who later became India's first prime minister – and many others, Gandhi believed that through *satyagraha* (non-violent protest) the pressure of the masses of Indian people on their British rulers would eventually lead to independence. Gandhi led many peaceful campaigns against British rule throughout the 1920s, 1930s, and 1940s. The British did grant

Mahatma ('the great soul') Gandhi (1869–1948)

Mahatma Gandhi was born in Gujarat in western India. As a young man he was a lawyer in London and South Africa. He returned to India in 1914 and soon became a leading figure in the Indian National Congress and the non-violent struggle for independence. He lived simply and led many protests, the biggest of which was the 322-kilometre (200-mile) 'Salt March' in 1930, protesting against high British taxes on salt. He was among 60,000 people jailed on this march.

Although beautiful silk, cotton, and wool cloth were made in India, the British took Indian raw materials back to their factories in England and then sold British-made cloth back to India. Gandhi encouraged the weaving and wearing of home-made (*khadi*) cloth so that Indian weavers would not lose their jobs. Even when he met King George V, Gandhi wore simple Indian handwoven cloth. In later life Gandhi was known as Mahatma 'great soul'. In January 1948, a few months after his dream of an independent India had been achieved, Gandhi was assassinated by a Hindu with very extreme views.

the Indians a certain amount of self-government during this period, but the demand for full independence continued.

The Muslim League

Indian politics at this time were further complicated by religious issues. Because most people in India were Hindus, the smaller number of Muslims feared that if India became independent it would turn into a Hindu state. They formed their own political movement, the Muslim League in 1906. From the 1930s there was increasing violence between Muslims and Hindus in India. Under its leader, Mohammed Ali Jinnah (1876–1948), the League campaigned for an independent Muslim state – Pakistan.

Jawaharlal Nehru (left) and Mahatma Gandhi at a meeting of the Indian Congress in 1946.

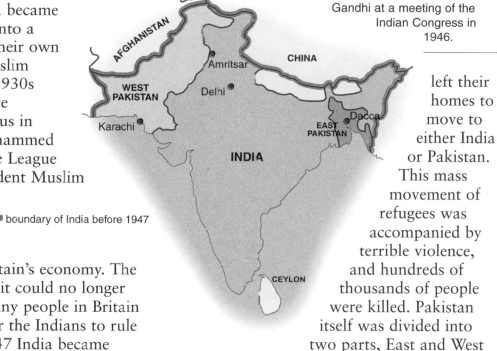

boundary of India before 1947

Independence

World War II exhausted Britain's economy. The British government decided it could no longer afford to rule India, and many people in Britain believed that it was right for the Indians to rule India. So, on 15 August 1947 India became independent, but as two separate states – Hindu India and Muslim Pakistan. At the time of Partition, as this division of British India is called, millions of Hindus, Muslims, and Sikhs left their homes to move to either India or Pakistan. This mass movement of refugees was accompanied by terrible violence, and hundreds of thousands of people were killed. Pakistan itself was divided into two parts, East and West Pakistan, separated by the new state of India. In 1971 East Pakistan became Bangladesh after fighting a war of independence against West Pakistan.

Israel: A Jewish Homeland

Zionism

In ancient times the Jewish people moved to Palestine, the 'Promised Land' of the Bible. Palestine was conquered by the Romans, who crushed a series of Jewish revolts. After this most Jews went into exile and ended up living in many parts of Europe, North Africa, and the Middle East. Jews were often persecuted – thrown out of their homes, forbidden to practise their religion, denied rights, and even killed. This hatred and persecution of Jews is known as anti-Semitism.

In the 19th century Jewish people started to think about the idea of a homeland for Jews – a place where they could live together and freely practise their religion – in Palestine. This movement became known as Zionism, named after Zion, one of the hills in ancient Jerusalem. Zionism was founded by an Austrian journalist called Theodor Herzl. In 1897 Herzl organized the first Zionist Congress, in Basel, Switzerland. Palestine was then part of the Turkish Ottoman Empire. When Herzl asked the Turkish government to grant Palestine independence as a Jewish homeland, the Turkish government refused. In 1905 the British government offered part of Uganda, in Africa, for the Jewish homeland, but the Zionists wanted Palestine. Later, in 1917, the British foreign minister Arthur Balfour said that the British government supported the idea of a Jewish homeland in Palestine.

Children are taught the history of their homeland in a kibbutz classroom.

Kibbutz

A kibbutz is a community in Israel where people live and work together, and land and property are owned jointly. Usually, the community is based around farming. The first kibbutz began in 1909 when Jewish immigrants in Palestine needed to work together to build houses and grow crops on the desert land. All the members of the kibbutz are treated the same and work to make the community run properly. Adults have their own bedrooms, but they share kitchens and dining rooms with other people in the community. Children stay together and some of the adults look after them and teach them in school. By the late 20th century there were more than 200 kibbutzes in Israel, with an average of 500 people living on each kibbutz.

After World War I, in which Britain defeated Turkey, Palestine came under British control.

In the early 20th century many Jewish people who were victims of anti-Semitism in Europe moved to Palestine. The Arabs who were already living in Palestine were not happy about Zionism, because they did not want their home to become a Jewish state where they would not be welcome. The persecution of Jewish people by the Nazis – who killed 6 million Jews during World War II – led to an increase in the number of Jewish people going to Palestine. Relations between the Arabs and the Zionists became even worse, and there were frequent violent clashes.

In 1947 the United Nations proposed a solution to the problem: to divide Palestine into Arab and Jewish areas. On 14 May 1948 the state of Israel was officially created for the Jews, with David Ben-Gurion as its first prime minister. The new state was immediately attacked by its Arab neighbours, the first of a number of wars between Jews and Arabs over land in the Middle East.

	proposed Jewish State
	proposed Arab State
	international area
——	boundary of Israel in 1948

Golda Meir (1898–1978)

Golda Meir was born in Russia but grew up in the USA. While she was a teenager she became a Zionist, and in 1921 she moved to Palestine. Throughout the 1930s and 1940s she served in various organizations working to make a Jewish state, and in 1948 she was one of the people who signed Israel's declaration of independence. She became active in politics and served as prime minister from 1969 to 1974. She worked very hard at trying to make peace between the Arabs and Jews in the Middle East. During this time she said: 'I honestly and sincerely believe that my grandchildren will live in an area of peace in the Middle East, because there are other grandmothers, in Egypt, and in Syria, and in Jordan, and they also want their grandchildren to live.' Golda Meir suffered from leukaemia, but was able to hide it until her death in 1978.

Golda Meir, one of the founders of the state of Israel. She was prime minister from 1969 to 1974.

The Dragon Stirs

China entered the 20th century with few industries, little wealth, and an outdated system of government based on the old systems created by the Manchu emperors. Lack of opportunity created unrest among many Chinese people, as did the influence of foreigners in their country who told them things could be different. In 1911 this unrest led to the overthrow of the emperor and to a change in government, with the creation of a Chinese republic in 1912. Those who had cooperated in removing the emperor then fell out among themselves.

The Struggle for Power

Yuan Shih-kai became president in 1912, but he did not do enough for those who had wanted to see real change in China. The ones who wanted change supported Sun Yat-sen and his party, known as the Kuomintang. Yuan died in 1916 and fighting developed between all the different groups who wanted power in China. While this was happening the Japanese helped themselves to the Chinese lands they wanted. Sun died in 1925 and was replaced as leader of the Kuomintang by Chiang Kai-shek. Chiang believed in firm government rather than in political change, and he tried to bring all of China under his control. He saw his main enemy as the Chinese communists and thought

that defeating them was even more important than driving out the Japanese. Chiang nearly succeeded, but the communists, led by Mao Zedong, managed to escape in the Long March.

The Last Emperor

There had been an emperor of China for over 2,000 years when in 1911 the country became a republic. Since 1644 the emperors had come from the Qing dynasty (ruling family) from Manchuria, a region of northeast China. The last emperor, Pu Yi, was a three-year-old boy when he came to the throne in 1908. He was deposed (removed from power) in 1912. After the Japanese had conquered Manchuria they renamed it Manchukuo, and in 1934 made Pu Yi emperor. After Japan was defeated in 1945, Pu Yi lived as a private citizen in Beijing, the capital of China, until he died.

Pu Yi, the last emperor of China. His short reign ended when he was just seven years old.

Mao Zedong (on horseback) leads his communist followers on their epic Long March through China.

The Long March

To the Chinese the real heroes of their communist revolution are those who took part in the Long March. In October 1934 the communists found themselves trapped by the Kuomintang in Hunan. The Kuomintang intended to starve them into surrender. An army of 100,000 communists, led by Mao Zedong, broke out of Hunan and wound their way through China, trying to avoid the Kuomintang, who attacked them whenever they could find them. The marchers met many hardships on their journey across deep river gorges, high mountain passes, and vast marshy grasslands. One year and 9,000 kilometres (5,600 miles) later they arrived in Yunan. Of the 100,000 who had set out, only 30,000 survived.

Chiang Kai-shek (1887–1975)

Chiang was a Chinese general who took over the leadership of the Kuomintang after the death of Sun Yat-sen. He was president of the Chinese Republic from 1928 to 1931 and again in 1948. When the Kuomintang lost to the communists in 1949, Chiang took his followers to the island of Taiwan and set up an anti-communist Chinese Republic there.

Sun Yat-sen (1866–1925)

While being educated abroad, where he qualified as a doctor, Sun picked up modern political ideas about democracy and socialism. He later formed the Kuomintang, a political party based on these ideas. After ten unsuccessful attempts at revolution, his ideas triumphed in 1911. Sun himself was out of the country at the time and never managed to get control of the revolution. He was appointed president of China in 1912 but resigned immediately in favour of Yuan Shih-kai. He died of cancer in 1925.

Meanwhile the Japanese were pushing further and further into China. In December 1941 the USA declared war on Japan in World War II, and by 1945 the Japanese were defeated. With Japan out of the way, fierce fighting broke out between the Kuomintang and the communists. The communists won and on 1 October 1949, Mao Zedong became chairman of the new People's Republic of China.

General Chiang Kai-shek, an anti-communist leader, stands beside the politician Sun Yat-sen. Chiang succeeded Sun as leader of the Kuomintang in 1925.

49

China under Communism

Communism is a political idea that says that the government, rather than individuals, owns the industries, and that the wealth of a country should be more evenly distributed. The communist People's Republic of China was established on 1 October 1949. Mao Zedong was its first chairman. Immediately, large privately owned landholdings were divided up and given to small peasant farmers, and the state took over ownership of industries, banks, newspapers, and radio stations. In the First Five-Year Plan (1953) farms were put into collective (shared) ownership. The Great Leap Forward (1958) divided China into communes, and everyone was urged to work very hard. People did, but there was no one properly in charge to organize them. This undirected hard work resulted in the production of less food and fewer goods, and there were terrible famines.

Posters like this encouraged the Chinese people to support Mao as their leader.

Mao Zedong (1893–1976)

Mao Zedong was the giant of the Chinese communist revolution. He realized that Chinese communism would have to be based on peasant farmers. This differed from the view of the German thinker Karl Marx, the founder of communism, who had said that the revolution would be based on factory workers. Without Mao's determined leadership the communists might not have won the civil war in 1949.

Mao was born in 1893 in Shao-shan, in Hunan province. In 1921 he helped set up the Chinese Communist Party. As first chairman of the People's Republic of China he developed communism as a form of government in China. In 1966, afraid of mounting opposition, he launched the Cultural Revolution. The resulting fear and chaos helped him regain control of the country. Mao died in 1976. In China he is known as 'the Great Helmsman' (a person who steers a ship) – but he also steered China into some very troubled waters from which the country is still returning.

Peking or Beijing?

The capital city of China can be spelt either way – why? The Chinese do not use our Roman alphabet. This makes it difficult for Westerners to read Chinese words. In the 19th century Sir Thomas Wade devised a system of transforming Chinese sounds into Roman letters. This system was later changed by Professor Herbert Giles. The Wade-Giles system of spelling Chinese words was used until the Chinese introduced their own system, Pinyin, in 1979. Peking is the Wade-Giles spelling, and Beijing is the Pinyin spelling.

The Cultural Revolution

Mao was blamed by other Chinese leaders for the failure of the Great Leap Forward. So in 1966 Mao launched the Cultural Revolution, which was an attempt to control everything and everybody in China. The Red Guard – made up of millions of teenagers who were fanatically loyal to Mao – were encouraged to attack and destroy everything that appeared old-fashioned, Western, or anti-communist. Schools and universities were closed down, and educated, skilled people such as teachers, government officials, and factory

Red Army soldiers read from the *Little Red Book* of Mao's writings.

Mao's *Little Red Book*

Quotations from the Works of Mao Zedong, published in 1966, was a small pocket-sized book with a red plastic cover. About 800 million copies of this *Little Red Book* were sold or given away between 1966 and 1971. To own it, read it, study it, and learn it was the sign of a good communist. Some people claimed that they literally never let it leave their hands.

A demonstration in Beijing in 1989 was ruthlessly crushed by the army.

managers were publicly humiliated and forced to go to the countryside to work on the land. When the revolution was ended in 1969 the Chinese people were exhausted and disillusioned. Those who wanted to lead China after Mao were struggling for power. The prime minister, Zhou Enlai, re-established the education system, encouraged the economy and, for the first time, promoted Chinese contacts with the outside world.

In 1976 both Mao and Zhou died. Mao's wife, Jiang Qing (part of a radical group that wanted power called the Gang of Four), tried to keep extreme Maoism going. But China's leaders preferred Deng Xiaoping, who favoured Zhou's moderate policies. Deng's aim was to modernize China and gives its 2 billion people a better life by the year 2000. He allowed workers in the factories and fields to make some of their own decisions and even to earn profits, and he also allowed private businesses. China began to settle down, and food production and factory output increased. This modernization did not include political freedom. In 1989 people demonstrated in many Chinese cities for greater freedom. On 3 June the army opened fire on a massive demonstration in Beijing's Tiananmen Square, and hundreds of demonstrators were killed. Deng died in 1997, leaving China ready for massive economic development in the 21st century.

Britain since 1945

The Start of the Welfare State

Following the defeat of Germany in World War II, a general election was held in July 1945. The Labour Party, under Clement Attlee, came to power with a large majority. The new government set up the Welfare State, which provided support for people in need 'from the cradle to the grave'. As part of the Welfare State, Labour created the National Health Service, which for the first time provided free health care for everybody. Labour also nationalized (brought under government ownership) many industries, such as the railways, coal, iron and steel, gas, and electricity, although later Conservative governments de-nationalized most of these.

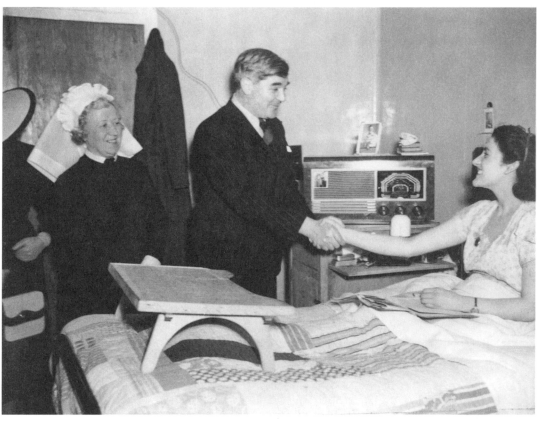

Aneurin Bevan was the Minister of Health responsible for setting up the National Health Service.

Economic Developments

Despite these changes, the years after the war were difficult for many people. Large parts of Britain's cities had been destroyed by German bombing, leaving many people without proper housing. Food and other goods were rationed for several years, and the shortage of housing continued to be a major problem into the 1960s. The cost of fighting the war had nearly bankrupted Britain, but from 1948 the country was helped by US financial aid under the Marshall Plan.

Britain's prosperity increased during the 1950s and 1960s, although there were problems. In the 1970s, a big increase in the price of oil, together with demands for higher wages led to high inflation, and many of Britain's industries found it difficult to compete in the world market. By 1982 more than 3 million people in Britain were unemployed. During the 1980s and earlier 1990s the Conservative governments of Margaret Thatcher and John Major brought about important changes in the British economy. They sold off many government-owned industries and services to private business, and reduced the power of the trade unions. Old and uncompetitive manufacturing industries declined, but the service industries (such as selling, insurance, banking, leisure, and tourism) became more important. The 'New Labour' government of Tony Blair, elected in 1997, largely left these economic changes in place, while seeking to support those less able to help themselves.

Britain's Changing Role

In 1945 Britain still ruled one of the largest empires the world has ever known. However, the cost of running this empire, together with a growing belief that the peoples in other countries should rule themselves, led Britain to

The late Princess Diana was one of the best-loved members of the Royal Family.

The Monarchy

Queen Elizabeth II is the official head of state and head of the Church of England, but has no political power. She has been queen since 1952 and people generally think she has done a difficult job well. The Queen, and other members of her family, represent Britain on many visits to foreign countries. They also do a great deal of valuable charity work.

Britain turned more and more to Europe. Its first application to join the European Economic Community (later the European Union) was turned down in 1963, but Britain eventually became a member in 1973. Both the main political parties – Conservatives and Labour – have been divided over just how far the British Parliament should hand over powers to Europe. Similar arguments have taken place over the devolution of power within the United Kingdom, but in 1997 the Scots voted in favour of a Scottish parliament, and the Welsh in favour of a Welsh assembly, both of which came into being in 1999.

withdraw from its colonies. India and Pakistan became independent in 1947, and during the 1950s and 1960s most of Britain's African colonies also gained their independence. By the end of the century the empire was reduced to a few small dependencies, although most of Britain's former colonies joined the Commonwealth of Nations, of which the Queen is the head.

Margaret Thatcher (here with her husband, Denis) was the 20th century's longest serving prime minister.

British Prime Ministers, 1945–2000

Prime Minister	Party	Years
Clement Attlee	Labour	1945–1951
Winston Churchill	Conservative	1951–1955
Anthony Eden	Conservative	1955–1957
Harold Macmillan	Conservative	1957–1963
Alec Douglas-Home	Conservative	1963–1964
Harold Wilson	Labour	1964–1970
Edward Heath	Conservative	1970–1974
Harold Wilson	Labour	1974–1976
James Callaghan	Labour	1976–1979
Margaret Thatcher	Conservative	1979–1990
John Major	Conservative	1990–1997
Tony Blair	Labour	1997–

The Changing Role of Women

In 1900 a woman's role was to look after home, husband, and children. It was difficult for women to get a good education, or even a job. The only country in the world where women could vote was New Zealand. Women had been given the right to vote there in 1893.

The Beginnings of Feminism

Women who seek the same rights and opportunities for women as for men are called feminists. During the late 18th century the Enlightenment in Europe was encouraging people to look beyond traditional beliefs and start thinking for themselves. During this time an Englishwoman called Mary Wollstonecraft published a book called *A Vindication of the Rights of Woman,* which says that women are not there just to please men and that they deserve the same rights in education, work, and voting. During the 19th century, women in Europe and the USA began to want equal rights and set up suffrage movements, demanding the right to vote. In 1903 the Women's Social and Political Union (WSPU) was formed by the

Emmeline Pankhurst, founder of the movement to fight for women's right to vote.

A policeman drags a suffragette protester away from Buckingham Palace.

famous English suffragette Emmeline Pankhurst and her daughters to demand votes for women. They were ignored, so some of these determined women burned buildings, refused to pay taxes, and chained themselves to railings to gain attention. In 1918 British women over 30 were given the vote as a reward for their work in World War I, and in 1928 they got equal voting rights with men.

Work and Education

At the beginning of the 20th century women were dependent on their husbands for money, and most of them did not work outside the home. However, things began to change. During both World War I and World War II women worked in the jobs left behind by men when they went to war. Women began to have fewer children, and new technologies for housekeeping, such as vacuum cleaners and washing machines, meant that women had more time. Women began to do the professional jobs traditionally reserved for men.

Liberation

In the 1960s women formed groups to demand liberation (freedom) to have equal opportunities with men. Many people think of this time as the height of the women's movement. In 1965 the US feminist Betty Friedan founded the National Organization for Women (NOW). Other organizations demanding equal rights for women quickly developed in the USA and Western Europe. Now women go to the best schools and universities, have high-powered jobs, and serve in governments, but they are still under represented.

Women cleaning the streets during World War I. This job would normally have been done by men.

In 1900 doctors claimed to have proved that women's brains were smaller and inferior to men's and so secondary education was considered a waste of time for girls. In 1944 all children got free secondary education, but girls did not do as well as boys in mixed schools, and nobody knew why. In the 1970s teachers began to understand that because girls were always being told that boys were better than them they did not try hard. They paid more attention to girls to give them more confidence. Now girls in the UK on average perform better in exams than boys.

The 1997 General Election saw many more women than before being elected to Parliament.

Simone de Beauvoir (1908–1986)

Simone de Beauvoir was a French writer, philosopher, and feminist. In 1949 she wrote a very famous book called *The Second Sex*. In this book she argued that people should be treated as individuals, and that people should forget traditional ideas about the differences between men and women. She argued that giving women freedom to follow their own goals would in turn give men more freedom too.

Women in the Third World

Women in the Third World have different ideas about what is important for them, and they are often part of a wider struggle for freedom for all their people. Many of these women are still subject to political or religious laws set by men that force them to dress a certain way or marry a certain person. Strong women everywhere – n Africa, Burma, India, South America – are struggling for human rights for their children, husbands, anc themselves.

Media and Communications

During the 20th century there was an explosion in communications. From sending messages by letter and getting news from the newspapers, the world moved to an age of instant global communications.

Messages down the Wire

The electric telegraph was the earliest method for instant communication. It used pulses of electricity sent along a wire. Early telegraphs used Morse code, a system of dots and dashes, to tap out messages, but later it became possible to type messages on a keyboard.

In 1873 Alexander Graham Bell transmitted sounds along a cable for the first time, and the telephone was born. Telephone systems caught on very quickly: by 1887 there were around 250,000 in use. At first they operated only locally, but soon there were countrywide telephone networks. The first telephone transmissions across the Atlantic Ocean were made in 1926.

Invisible Beams

The next step in the communications revolution did away with wires. Radio waves were discovered in the late 19th century. A young Italian, Guglielmo Marconi, saw that they could be used to send messages, and in 1896 he built a 'wireless apparatus' that could send Morse code messages. By 1901 he could send messages across the Atlantic. The first sound broadcast was made in 1906, and in the 1920s the first radio stations began broadcasting. In the USA radio stations made their money from advertising. In Britain the government set up the British Broadcasting Corporation (the BBC), which was paid for by charging radio owners a licence fee.

Television, which also uses radio waves to send signals, followed soon after radio. The first practical television system was developed in the 1930s, and in 1936 the BBC made its first television broadcasts. Early television pictures were black and white; colour television became available in the USA in the 1950s. From the 1950s programmes were recorded on videotape, and in the 1970s the first home video recorders went on sale.

A family gathers round their black-and-white television set in the 1950s.

Getting the News

When radio and then television broadcasts began, newspapers were no longer first with the news. Some newspapers closed, while others became part of huge media groups that also included radio and television stations. Newspapers competed with radio and television by investigating stories in more depth than was possible in a radio or television report. They also entertained their readers with competitions, cartoons, and celebrity stories.

Going Global

In the 1980s telephone networks began to send sound signals digitally (as strings of binary numbers). This improved the quality of calls and made it possible to send many calls down the same line. Optical fibres, which can carry huge numbers of telephone calls or radio or television signals, began to be used in the mid-1980s. Using a combination of communication satellites, cables, optical fibres, radio waves, and microwaves (very short radio waves), telephone calls, faxes, e-mails, and radio and television broadcasts can now be transmitted almost instantly from one side of the world to the other.

Fibre optic cables can carry much more information than the copper wires that were first used to carry telephone messages.

An artist's impression of a communications satellite in orbit around the Earth.

Sounds Good

The first sound-recording machines recorded mechanically, using a large horn to concentrate the sound. Much better quality came in the 1920s with electrical recording, using a microphone, an amplifier, and loudspeakers. The first tape recorders appeared in the 1930s. They were soon in use for professional recording, but it was the cassette tape, introduced in the 1960s, that made tape players popular in homes. The compact disc (CD) was developed in the early 1980s. CD recordings are digital: the sound is not recorded directly, but as a string of binary numbers. In the 1990s several other kinds of digital recording media were developed, including digital audio tape (DAT) and the minidisc.

Pirate Radio

In Britain private radio stations were not allowed for many years. Then in the 1960s 'pirate' radio stations, operating illegally, began to broadcast pop music. Often they were based on ships just offshore. Millions of young people tuned in to the pirate stations, and their popularity led to the introduction of commercial radio during the 1970s.

Fashion in the 20th Century

From Corsets to Flappers

Clothes changed enormously during the 20th century. Shapes and styles of clothes can tell you about the changes that are happening in a country and the way they influence people.

In the Edwardian era (1901–1910) the fashionable woman was shaped like an hour-glass with a large bust and hips and a very small waist. She achieved this with the aid of a corset (stiffened with whalebone) under her petticoats and long flowing skirts. Dresses were covered in lace and braid and the huge hats were decorated with feathers, flowers, beads, and lace. Meanwhile, men mostly wore suits. Professional men wore frock coats with striped or check trousers and a top hat to work, while ordinary office workers such as clerks favoured the lounge suit.

In the second decade (1911–1920) women were insisting on more freedom and demanding the vote. They started playing more sports and clothing became looser. The whalebone corset was on its way out. During World War I (1914–1918), with so many men away fighting, women were allowed to work at many jobs previously only done by men. Their new role was reflected in more comfortable clothing. The shorter, fuller skirts and long loose jackets of 1918 were businesslike and comfortable.

The post-war freedom of the 1920s brought new, softer, straighter styles. Flappers – young women with shorter, knee-length skirts, flat chests, and boyish bobbed hair – appeared in 1925. It was the first time so much female leg had been shown. Hemlines moved back to the knee by 1928. When not in the office, middle-class men wore tweed sports jackets and flannel trousers. 'Oxford bags' (trousers with very wide legs) and 'plus fours' (baggy knee-length breeches) were fashionable.

Poverty and Rationing

The 1930s brought economic depression and poverty, and more sensible adult clothing. Skirts fell to mid-calf and were gently flared with a natural waistline. Evening dresses were floor-length and flowing, made from silk chiffon and new materials such as lamé (fabric with threads of metal woven into it).

During World War II (1939–1945) cloth was rationed and people had to choose sensible clothing. Skirts got shorter, men gave up their waistcoats, and there were no fancy frills anywhere. Women started wearing trousers.

Fuller Fifties and Swinging Sixties

The period after the war (1946–1960) showed a return to a more womanly form and was dominated by the shape of Christian Dior's 'New Look', with tightly fitting tops and below-the-knee full skirts. In the 1950s young women stiffened their petticoats with sugar to make their

A woman models the Flapper style of dress that was popular in the 1920s.

58

Rock 'n' Roll idol Elvis Presley in the clean-cut college style worn by many men in the 1950s.

Punk and Piercings

From the mid-1970s many young people rejected the softness of hippydom. They started to wear slashed jeans, holey T-shirts, and safety pins through their noses, and to have spikey hairstyles. Street fashion created by young people was copied by designers.

The 1980s and 1990s continued this freedom in fashion. In the 1980s 'power dressing' for the office was offset by pretty, frivolous clothes and shell suits for leisure. There was a fashion, perhaps started by Madonna, for corsets to be worn on the outside of your clothes. In the 1990s piercings and tattoos became very popular for many teenagers.

skirts stick out, which was a problem if you got caught in the rain! Teddy boys appeared in the 1950s, wearing drape jackets with velvet collars, drainpipe trousers, crepe-soled shoes, and their hair slicked back.

The early 1960s saw the advent of the miniskirt. Designers took on the ideas from spacesuits – making short dresses and short boots out of plastic and other unusual fabrics. In the later 1960s hippies began creating their own look with flared trousers, flowing kaftans, embroidery, and beads.

The Swimming Costume

People began to wear swimming costumes in the mid-19th century, when railways made it easier to get to the seaside. The first swimming costumes covered most of the body. Women wore bloomers, black stockings, and a dress. Men wore a dark-coloured one-piece suit reaching the knees or ankles. By the early 20th century men had begun to wear shorts without a top. After World War I a tighter-fitting one-piece swimsuit for women was introduced in France, and in 1947 the bikini came into fashion. By the end of the century men and women had a greater choice in styles and fabrics that would be comfortable in the water and dry quickly.

Fashion designers and 'supermodels', like Naomi Campbell here, attract a lot of press attention.

The Cold War

The Cold War is the name given to the hostility that existed from 1945 to 1990 between the Union of Soviet Socialist Republics (USSR or Soviet Union) and its communist allies on one side, and the democracies of Western Europe and North America on the other. It was called the 'Cold War' because the main countries involved did not actually go to war with each other, although they did go to war against some of each other's allies. To increase their power, both the USSR and the USA tried to influence less powerful countries. The USSR tried to spread communism, while the USA tried to stop it.

The Beginning of the Cold War

Ever since the communists had come to power in the Russian Revolution in 1917, the West had not trusted the USSR. The USA and the USSR had become allies in World War II in order to defeat Nazi Germany, but at the end of the war in 1945 the Soviet dictator Joseph Stalin insisted on controlling the countries of Eastern Europe that his armies had freed from the Nazis. Over 20 million Soviets had died in the war with Germany, and the USSR wanted a barrier of friendly countries between itself and its former enemy. The Soviets set up communist governments in these countries, and anybody who opposed these governments was treated harshly. Winston Churchill said that an 'Iron Curtain' had fallen across Europe.

A military parade in Moscow's Red Square during the May Day celebrations. The huge banner shows Lenin, Engels, and Marx.

Germany and the Berlin Wall

At the end of World War II Germany had been divided into four occupation zones. The western zones were governed by the USA, Britain, and France, while the eastern zone was governed by the USSR. The German capital, Berlin, was divided in the same way. In 1948 the Soviet dictator Joseph Stalin tried to take over the Western part of Berlin by stopping all supplies from entering the city, but he did not succeed. The following year Germany was divided into two new countries: democratic West Germany and communist East Germany. Berlin again became the centre of world attention in 1961 when the Soviets built a line of concrete barriers through the city, the 'Berlin Wall', to stop East Germans fleeing to the West. As the Soviet empire began to crumble in 1989, the East German authorities themselves broke down the wall, and in the following year East and West Germany were reunited.

In the USA the government saw Stalin's actions as a move towards trying to conquer the world, and determined to resist the spread of communism. The USA gave money to Western European countries, to help them rebuild their shattered economies, and to protect them against communist takeover.

In 1949 the North Atlantic Treaty Organization (NATO) was formed. This was a military alliance of the USA, Canada, and most of the countries of Western Europe, for mutual defence against the threat of communism. In 1955 the USSR and Eastern European communist countries joined to form the Warsaw Pact.

The Nuclear Threat

After World War II both the USA and the USSR developed more and more powerful nuclear weapons, together with missiles that could carry the bombs and hit cities on the other side of the world. Both sides realized that if they were to use these weapons, the other side would retaliate, and both sides would be completely destroyed. The existence of nuclear weapons was one of the reasons the two sides never went to war. Eventually a number of treaties were signed to reduce the number of nuclear weapons.

President John F Kennedy addressing a news conference after the Cuban missile crisis had been resolved.

John F Kennedy and the Cuban Missile Crisis

John F Kennedy (1917–1963) was president of the USA from 1961 to 1963. At home he introduced far-reaching reforms, helping those who were under-privileged, or who suffered racial discrimination. In international affairs he took one of the biggest risks of the Cold War.

In 1959 Fidel Castro came to power in Cuba, an island in the Caribbean just south of the USA. Castro took over industries owned by US companies, so in 1961 Kennedy backed an invasion by anti-Castro Cubans, which was defeated at the Bay of Pigs. After this Castro allied himself closely with the USSR, and in 1962 allowed Soviet missiles to be based in Cuba. Kennedy set up a naval blockade of the island, and told the Soviet leader Nikita Khruschev that the USA would use nuclear weapons unless the missiles were removed. For a short period the world feared that nuclear war was about to break out, but in the end the Soviets took away the missiles.

After this, both sides tried to reduce the tension between them. In 1963 Kennedy helped bring about the signing of a nuclear test ban treaty between the USA, USSR, and Britain. In November of the same year he was assassinated in Dallas, Texas.

The End of the Cold War

The USA was a much richer country than the USSR, and could develop ever more expensive military technology. The USSR's attempt to keep up with the USA put a great strain on its economy. When a new Soviet leader, Mikhail Gorbachev, came to power in 1985, he realized something must change. He encouraged political and economic reforms within the USSR and its allies, and improved relations with the West. In 1989 the communist governments of Eastern Europe were replaced by democratically elected governments. The republics that made up the USSR (including the biggest, Russia) also began to break away from the central control of the Soviet Communist Party. By the end of 1991 the USSR no longer existed, and the Cold War had come to an end.

The Korean War

In 1950 communist North Korea invaded capitalist South Korea. A war followed in which the United Nations – chiefly the USA – supported South Korea, and communist China supported the North. Finally, in 1953, after long peace talks, the war ended, with boundaries restored as they had been before.

A US army mortar crew fires on communist forces during the Korean War.

The Vietnam War

Communism in Vietman

Vietnam used to be a colony of France. Together with Cambodia and Laos, it was part of French Indochina. During World War II Vietnam was occupied by the Japanese. The communist leader Ho Chi Minh organized resistance to the Japanese, and declared Vietnam independent from France in 1945. The French refused to accept Ho Chi Minh's communist government, and war broke out between the two countries, ending in a French defeat in 1954. In a peace treaty signed that year, the French granted independence to Cambodia and Laos, and Vietnam was divided into two independent countries: North Vietnam, ruled by Ho Chi Minh's communist government, and South Vietnam. The USA supported South Vietnam because it was seen as a strategic place from which to try to stop the spread of communism into the rest of Southeast Asia.

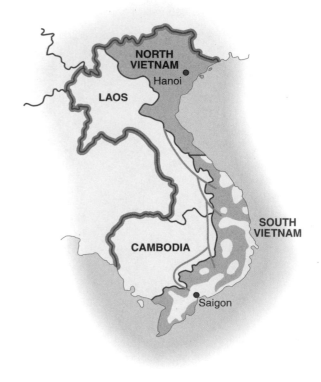

■■■ French - Indochina

▨ area under communist control 1946–1954

—— Ho Chi Minh Trail

North and South Vietnam were never friendly neighbours. Ho Chi Minh was determined to reunite Vietnam under communist rule. The South Vietnamese government also struggled against communist rebels, called the Vietcong, at home. As fighting increased, the USA sent military supplies and advisers to help South Vietnam.

The USA Enters the War

US troops landed in South Vietnam in early 1965 to help fight the North

American troops were airlifted into battle by helicopters.

62

Anti-War Protests

People in the USA and around the world quickly began to object to the Vietnam War. For one thing, in the USA there was a system called the draft, which forced men as young as 18 to go and fight in a war that many of them did not believe in. Many of them died. For another thing, people could see what was going on because it was the first war to be widely covered on television. US troops killed many Vietnamese peasants, mistaking them for disguised Vietcong. They also bombed villages with napalm, a chemical that sticks to the skin and burns, and sprayed poisonous chemicals on the forests to kill the trees so the Vietcong had nowhere to hide.

In 1966 the first anti-war demonstrations took place in the USA. By the following year, protests were taking place all over the world. Music, literature, and clothing reflected the growing anti-Vietnam War culture, particularly among young people in the USA. The US president Lyndon B Johnson became so unpopular that he decided not to run for re-election in 1968. The anti-war feeling helped persuade the new president, Richard Nixon, to withdraw the USA from the war.

The Tet Offensive and After

The North Vietnamese and Vietcong forces launched a major attack on the South Vietnamese and US forces on 30 January 1968. Called the Tet Offensive, it was unsuccessful, but the power of the much smaller North Vietnamese and Vietcong forces convinced the USA that the war was not going to be easily won.

Vietnamese and Vietcong rebels. By the end of 1965 nearly 400,000 Americans, Australians, and New Zealanders were fighting in Vietnam.

The USA thought that they could fight a traditional war, with large-scale battles between the two sides, but the Vietcong's guerrilla tactics made it very difficult for them. Firstly, the Vietcong moved around in small groups, avoiding open battles. Secondly, they were experts at hiding from the US soldiers. One way was to dress as ordinary peasants by day and launch attacks under the cover of night. Another method was digging a network of secret tunnels, from which they were able to make surprise attacks. The USA began bombing weapons sites in North Vietnam, hoping to cut off the supply to the Vietcong in South Vietnam, but the North Vietnamese continued to receive a large amount of supplies from the Soviet Union and China.

The Americans and the North Vietnamese began peace negotiations in 1968, but the fighting continued. In 1970 the USA bombed and invaded Cambodia, intending to cut off Vietcong supply lines (the Ho Chi Minh trail), but in the process around 1 million Cambodians were killed or wounded. The growing opposition to the war back in the USA persuaded the US government to withdraw its forces. The last US troops finally left in 1973, but fighting continued until 1975 when the North Vietnamese took over South Vietnam and the two countries were reunited.

Captured Vietcong are lead off for questioning by an American soldier.

Africa: The Winds of Change

Freedom!

At the end of the 19th century, in a scramble for new territory, the African continent had been divided up among several European countries. The Europeans wanted Africa for the raw materials they needed for their industries. During the 20th century the peoples of Africa began to fight back. They felt like foreigners in their own countries and they wanted their own governments. There were demonstrations and riots in the streets. In Kenya a guerrilla army called the Mau Mau fought against the British

South Africa – The End of Apartheid

In South Africa more than three-quarters of the people are black, Asian, or coloured (of mixed race), and the small remainder are white. The white minority are a mixture of English-speakers and Afrikaners (Afrikaans-speaking descendants of Dutch settlers). After becoming independent in 1910 South Africa always had a white government. Non-whites were not allowed to stand for parliament or to vote.

Mau Mau prisoners surrounded by barbed wire in a prison camp outside Nairobi.

farmers who had taken their land. In Algeria there was a violent war against the French colonists. There were wars of independence against the Europeans in a number of other countries, but in most of Africa independence was achieved peacefully. The first African country to gain independence was Ghana in 1957. The last country to gain independence was Rhodesia (now called Zimbabwe) in 1980.

Afraid that the black majority would take over the country, after World War II the white government introduced a system called apartheid. Apartheid means 'separateness' in Afrikaans. It meant that white and non-white people were not allowed to live in the same areas, go to school together, marry each other, sit on the same bus, or mix in many other ways. Black people had to carry passes to show who they were and were not allowed to walk around in freedom. Many people who broke

Nelson Mandela was born the son of a Xhosa chief. He spent his boyhood herding cattle. Later he went to university in Johannesburg, becoming a lawyer and setting up South Africa's first black legal practice. In 1964 he was sentenced to life imprisonment. In 1990 the South African president FW de Klerk ended the ban on the ANC and released Mandela from jail. After becoming the first black president of South Africa in 1994, Mandela did much to bring black and white people together and to put an end to years of bitterness. He shared the Nobel Prize for Peace in 1993 with President FW de Klerk.

campaign against it. It held strikes, rallies, and demonstrations, until the government banned the ANC in 1960. Realizing that this peaceful campaign was not altering the government's attitude, in 1961 ANC Youth League leader and lawyer Nelson Mandela and others formed the Umkhonto we Sizwe (Spear of the Nation) guerrilla army to try to get something done. Mandela, Walter Sisulu and others were jailed for life on Robben Island in 1964 for violent acts.

Over the years (even though the apartheid government called him a terrorist) Nelson Mandela became popular around the world and was seen as the leader of the black people of South Africa. Pressure from within South Africa and the rest of the world led to his release in 1990, after 27 years. In 1993 Mandela and the last white president of South Africa, F W de Klerk, won the Nobel Peace Prize for ending apartheid. In April 1994, in the first election in which black people could vote, Mandela became South Africa's first black president.

the laws or spoke out against apartheid were tortured and killed. Others were kept under house arrest for years and not allowed to speak to anyone.

Families and Apartheid

Apartheid ripped black families apart. Wives and children lived in homelands (poorer areas of the country given to blacks) while husbands went to town to work in mines and factories – often not returning home for over a year. Many women worked as nannies for white children and never saw their own children.

The African National Congress and Nelson Mandela

The African National Congress (ANC) was formed in 1912 to campaign for rights for non-white people. After the introduction of apartheid the ANC led a peaceful

F W de Klerk and Nelson Mandela celebrate the end of apartheid in South Africa.

Conflict in the Middle East

The State of Israel

The modern state of Israel was founded in Palestine in 1948. The United Nations (UN) decided that dividing Palestine into two parts, one for Jews and one for Arabs, was a good way to make peace in the area. But neither the Jews nor the Arabs were happy about the division of the land. Armies from the surrounding Arab countries entered Palestine. The Israeli army fought back, winning over three-quarters of Palestine.

After the war, 750,000 Palestinians had to leave Israeli territory. They went to Jordan, Gaza, Lebanon, and Syria. In 1949 the UN set up refugee camps, where the Palestinians lived in miserable conditions. They all wanted to go home; most kept the key to their houses.

The Arab countries fought Israel several times to try to win back land, but they failed. In 1967 Israel won more land, including the West Bank and Gaza Strip, where many Palestinian refugees lived. In 1987 the Palestinians began an uprising against Israel. It continued until the peace process of the early 1990s.

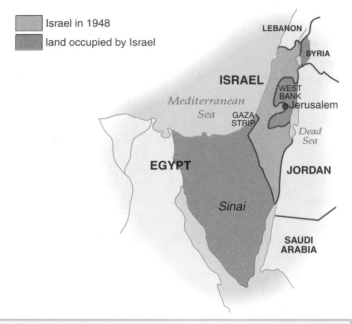

Israel in 1948

land occupied by Israel

Main Arab–Israeli Wars	
1948–1949	Egypt, Jordan, Iraq, Syria, and Lebanon invade Israel. Israel defeats them.
1956	Egypt nationalizes the British- and French-owned Suez Canal. Britain, France, and Israel agree to attack Egypt, but are forced to withdraw.
1967	Six-Day War. Israel fights against Egypt, Syria, and Jordan. Israel gains Arab Jerusalem, the West Bank, Gaza Strip, Sinai, and Golan Heights.
1973	Yom Kippur War. Egypt and Syria attack Israel.
1979	Israel and Egypt make peace, and Israel returns Sinai.
1982–1985	Israel invades Lebanon and becomes involved in the Lebanese civil war.

Allied armoured vehicles go into battle during the Gulf War.

The Gulf War

There have been many other conflicts in the Middle East. Between 1980 and 1988 Iraq and Iran fought a bitter war over territory, which cost 1 million lives. Another major war, the Gulf War, broke out in the Persian Gulf region after Saddam Hussein sent his Iraqi troops into Kuwait in August 1990. The world was shocked and also worried, because much of the world's oil supplies came from Kuwait. In January 1991 an international force, organized by the UN, led by the USA, and including many Britons, bombed Iraq. The following month a quick land campaign successfully drove the Iraqi army out of Kuwait. No one knows how many Iraqi soldiers died – maybe as many as 100,000. The UN forces lost 300 soldiers.

The 1990s Peace Process

The USA arranged a conference with Israeli and Arab leaders in 1991. They agreed to help make peace between Israel and its Arab neighbours, and the Palestinians. In 1993 a peace agreement was signed in the USA. The Palestinian leader Yasser Arafat agreed that Israel should have the right to exist. Israel said it would begin to move out of the West Bank and Gaza Strip and let the Palestinians run their own affairs. The Israeli foreign minister Shimon Peres remembers that '[Israeli prime minister] Rabin didn't want to shake Arafat's hand. It was terrible. The whole world was watching...' Finally he did, and the difficult peace process began.

Prime Minister Rabin of Israel and Palestinian leader Yasser Arafat shake hands watched by US president Bill Clinton.

Yitzhak Rabin (1922–1995)

Yitzhak Rabin served in World War II and developed many skills that made him an excellent military leader. He became the chief of staff of Israel's army in 1964 and planned the strategy that helped Israel win the Six-Day War of 1967. Later he entered politics and became prime minister in 1974 and again in 1992. His government began the secret talks that led to the peace agreement of 1993, for which he, Yasser Arafat, and Shimon Peres won the Nobel Peace Prize. In 1995 he was killed by a young Jewish extremist who was against the whole peace process.

Yasser Arafat (1929–)

Yasser Arafat became chairman of the Palestinian Liberation Organization (PLC) in 1969. The PLO wanted to return Israel to the Palestinians. Arafat used terrorism (acts of violence for political reasons) and also tried to persuade the world to help the Palestinians. He ran the PLO from different Arab countries, often moving because the rulers did not want the PLO there. In 1994, after the peace agreement, he moved to Gaza to lead the Palestinian-ruled parts of the West Bank and Gaza Strip. He was elected president of the Palestinian Authority in 1996.

Ireland

The Creation of the Irish Free State

The question of Home Rule bitterly divided the Irish people at the beginning of the 20th century. Unionists, mainly Protestants in the northern province of Ulster, wanted to remain part of Great Britain, and nationalists, mainly Roman Catholics, wanted complete independence from Great Britain. In the summer of 1914 Ireland was close to civil war. This was only avoided by the outbreak of a general war in Europe, the start of World War I. The majority of Irish people, whatever their religion or politics, decided to join Britain and the Allies in the war against Germany.

On 24 April 1916, Easter Monday, 1,600 armed volunteers, led by Padraic Pearse, captured the main post office in Dublin and declared an Irish Republic. They held out against government forces for four days. Afterwards nearly 3,500 people were arrested, and 15 people, including Pearse, were executed. However, the execution of the leaders, and the sight of Irish republicans successfully resisting the government, created many more republican supporters.

In the British general election of 1918, the republican party of Sinn Féin won 73 out of a total of 105 Irish seats. The 73 winners refused to go to Westminster, and set up their own parliament in Dublin instead. A campaign of violence was launched, led by Éamon de Valera and Michael Collins, to force the government to recognize an Irish republic.

A separate province of Northern Ireland, formed out of six northern counties, was created in 1920, with its own parliament at Stormont. Today Northern Ireland remains part of the United Kingdom. The Anglo-Irish Treaty of 1921 established the Irish Free State, but this was part of the British Commonwealth, and not the independent republic that many Irish nationalists wanted. They wanted the whole island, not just part of it, to be under Irish rule. Civil war broke out between pro- and anti-treaty nationalists. Finally there was a ceasefire in 1923. The Republic of Ireland was established in 1949, and left the Commonwealth.

Northern Ireland: The Troubles

In 1968 the Catholic minority in Northern Ireland began to campaign for equal rights with the Protestant majority. The Catholics had suffered discrimination for many years in areas such as housing, voting, and employment. Northern Ireland was on the brink of civil war in 1969, and British troops were sent in to keep

British troops became a common sight on the streets of Northern Ireland.

the two sides apart. As a result, the Provisional IRA (Irish Republican Army) opened a campaign of violence against Protestants, the police, and the army. Protestant groups fought back and in March 1972 the British government decided to rule Northern Ireland directly from London. The bombings and murders spread to mainland Britain. The car

David Trimble (left) and John Hume (right) won the Nobel Peace Prize in 1998.

bomb became a favourite weapon and terrible atrocities (cruel and violent acts) were committed by both sides in the conflict. Thousands of people have been maimed or killed in Northern Ireland since the start of the troubles.

The British government believed that cooperation with the government of the Irish Republic would help find a solution. This approach eventually led to the Good Friday Agreement of 10 April 1998, bringing hope of a permanent settlement to the situation in Northern Ireland. The leaders of the two main opposing parties in Northern Ireland, the nationalist John Hume and the unionist David Trimble, who had always before been enemies, won the Nobel Peace Prize for their work towards the peace agreement.

At midnight on 1 December 1999 the responsibility for governing Northern Ireland

was transferred from Westminster to a new power-sharing executive. This executive is made up of both nationalist and unionist politicians and has responsibility for areas such as health, education, and housing. Tony Blair, the British prime minister, said "There are going to be many difficulties along the way to achieving a lasting peace in Northern Ireland but I believe one huge, giant step forward has been taken".

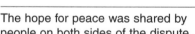

The hope for peace was shared by people on both sides of the dispute.

Did You Know?

Ireland's ancient Gaelic language is still spoken in parts of Ireland and is used for some political names and titles.

Taoiseach	prime minister
Dáil Eireann	Irish Parliament
Teachtai Dala	member of Parliament
Fianna Fáil	Warriors of Ireland
Fine Gael	the Irish Race
Sinn Féin	ourselves alone

Space: The New Frontier

Until the 20th century space exploration was something that was only imagined in books. But after World War I rocket technology developed rapidly, and by 1969 rockets were powerful enough to carry the first people to the Moon.

Early Rockets

The father of modern rocketry was the US scientist Robert Goddard, who launched the first liquid-fuelled rocket in 1926. During World War II, German researchers under Wernher von Braun developed more powerful rockets.

The space shuttle Columbia lifts off from the Kennedy Space Centre.

Edwin Aldrin on the Moon. There have been no Moon landings since 1972.

The most advanced of these was the V-2, which could carry 750 kilograms of explosive faster than the speed of sound. After the war, researchers in the USA and the USSR built rocket-powered missiles that could go much greater distances.

A US astronaut walking in space. The first man to walk in space was Soviet cosmonaut Aleksi Leonov in March 1965.

Edwin Hubble (1889–1953)

Edwin Hubble was the one of the greatest astronomers of the century. He was the first to demonstrate that these are other galaxies beyond our own Milky Way and that the universe was much larger than had been thought. He also made the discovery that these other galaxies are moving apart from each other – suggesting that the universe is expanding, and that it started with a 'Big Bang'. In 1990 a powerful optical telescope was carried into space. It was named the Hubble telescope in honour of Edwin Hubble.

The Space Race

In 1957 the USSR launched the first artificial satellite, Sputnik 1, into orbit around the Earth. This began a 'space race' between the USA and the USSR. In 1961 the Russian Yuri Gagarin became the first human to orbit the Earth; the US astronaut John Glenn did so in 1962. Rapid advances were made – soon spacecraft were meeting in orbit, and astronauts walked in space. By 1966 the USSR had landed an unmanned spacecraft on the Moon, but the USA concentrated on putting the first 'man on the Moon'. In 1969 the spacecraft Apollo 11 took three astronauts to the Moon, and Neil Armstrong and Edwin 'Buzz' Aldrin became the first humans to walk on its surface.

Deep-Space Probes

After the Moon landing, the focus of space exploration shifted to unmanned deep-space probes. The Soviet Venera space probes sent back images and information from the surface of Venus, while the US Viking 1 and 2 landed on Mars, and the two US Voyager probes flew past Jupiter, Saturn, Uranus, and Neptune. The Galileo probe reached Jupiter in 1995. It

Discoveries in Astronomy

Astronomers learned a great deal about space in the 20th century from powerful new types of telescope. As well as sending out light, stars and galaxies send out other kinds of radiation, such as X-rays and radio waves. Using telescopes that detect these rays, scientists have discovered new kinds of objects in space. Pulsars, for example, send out powerful, rapidly pulsing radio signals. They are thought to be spinning neutron stars, the dark and very dense remains of stars that have reached the end of their life.

Space Stations

Space stations orbiting the Earth have been used by scientists to carry out experiments in the zero-gravity conditions of space. The first space station was the Soviet Salyut I, which went into orbit in 1971. In 1986 the USSR launched a much larger space station, Mir. Scientists from all over the world have carried out experiments there. A new International Space Station is now being built. The first parts were assembled in space in 1998.

discovered the possible presence of a liquid ocean beneath the icy surface of Europa, one of Jupiter's moons. Lunar Prospector, a probe launched in 1998 to study the Moon, found millions of tonnes of ice scattered across its north and south poles.

The Rise of Asia

Asia is the largest continent in the world and one of the most varied. At the end of the 20th century some of its people, in countries such as Bangladesh and Myanmar (formerly Burma), were suffering poverty and oppression. Others lived in ultra-modern countries, such as Singapore and Japan, and enjoyed very high standards of living.

richer country or region

poorer country

The Tiger Economies

In the Middle East (western Asia), where more than three-quarters of Asia's oil reserves are found, wealth comes from the production and export of petroleum. Economic growth in Southeast Asia is mostly based on having a lot of industries that make and sell an enormous number of consumer goods. Japan's has been the most spectacular success story, but other countries have almost equalled its progress. Hong Kong, Singapore, Taiwan, and South Korea are known as the 'Four Tigers' because of their success in becoming very important trading nations. They are named after tigers because tigers are aggressive. Other 'tiger' economies include Malaysia, Indonesia, and Thailand. Economists called the rapid growth in these countries the 'Asian Miracle'.

Economic Crisis

In the late 1990s Southeast Asia suffered an economic crisis of gigantic proportions. It started in July 1997 when the value of national currencies dropped in Thailand, Malaysia, Indonesia, and South Korea. At the same time exports dropped to half of what they had been

in 1994 and 1995. This made it difficult for Asian businesses to pay back loans they owed in dollars and other foreign currencies. The banks that had financed these loans were left with very little money and on the brink of collapse. The governments of South Korea, Indonesia, and Thailand were rescued by loans from several other Asian countries and the International Monetary Fund (IMF), an organization set up to protect major currencies. However, confidence in the Asian economy suffered, and people around the world who had investments in Asian firms lost money.

Poor Countries

At the end of the 20th century most of the people living in less-developed regions in Asia were unable to get modern medical care. Malnutrition (poor diet) and disease were common. In some countries the average lifespan was only 45, compared with Japan and Taiwan, where the average person lived to the age of 70 or more.

Singapore

A country's economy is judged to be weak or strong by how much money the country as a whole makes. The Singaporean economy has grown steadily since the 1960s, and at the end of the 20th century Singapore had the strongest economy of any country in Southeast Asia. Much of Singapore's wealth is made from international trade, high finance, oil refining, and high-technology industries such as electronics.

Hong Kong

Like Japan, Hong Kong was devastated during World War II. The economy improved somewhat during the 1950s and 1960s when inexpensive goods such as textiles were exported to the world market. But these industries relied on sweatshops. These were small factories where people worked long hours for low wages. The workers rebelled in the late 1960s, staging violent political demonstrations that forced the government to improve living and working conditions generally. At the same time, many people grew rich from the new high-technology industries and growing foreign investment.

On 1 July 1997 Hong Kong was formally handed over to the People's Republic of China after 165 years as a British colony. An agreement signed by Britain and China 13 years earlier specified that China could not interfere with Hong Kong's way of life until 2047, but some people in Hong Kong feared that China would try to limit their rights and freedoms.

The Hong Kong skyline at night.

Japan

In 1945, at the end of World War II, much of Japan was in ruins. Its cities had been devastated by US bombing, including the dropping of atomic bombs on Hiroshima and Nagasaki. With help from the USA, Japan made radical changes to its political, educational, and social systems, and transformed itself into a modern democratic state. The latest technology was employed to build new factories and communications and transport systems. By the 1980s Japan had become one of the largest economic powers in the world. Demand for its cars, electrical goods, and computer technology was so high that Japan manufactured and sold one-tenth of the world's total output of these products.

A computer-controlled Japanese car production line.

The Decline of Communism

The Collapse of Communism in Europe

In 1980, in a Polish shipyard, a group called Solidarity was formed. It was a union of workers who were protesting against recent massive rises in food prices under communist rule. This marked the beginning of the downfall of European communism. In 1981 Solidarity was banned and its leader, Lech Wałęsa, imprisoned – but it remained active in secret. In 1988 more price rises and low wages caused strikes all over Poland. Solidarity banners flew, and the government had to recognize the banned union. In 1989 free elections were held, and Solidarity triumphed. By 1990 the communists had gone, and Lech Wałęsa became president.

Events in Poland, along with the reforming attitude of the Soviet president Mikhail Gorbachev, inspired similar movements in other Eastern European countries. By 1991 the whole of Eastern Europe was free from the restrictions of single-party communist rule.

Lech Wałęsa, leader of the Polish Solidarity movement.

The Berlin Wall Comes Down

The Berlin Wall was built in 1961, across the heart of the German capital city. Those who found themselves on the communist Eastern side were banned from crossing to the West, even if relatives were there. Anyone who tried to cross was shot and left to die.

People gather to tear down the Berlin Wall in 1989.

In 1989 many Eastern European countries were allowing people to leave, recognizing a movement that was too powerful to stop. On 9 November 1989 it was announced that the Berlin Wall was no longer a barrier to freedom. People gathered in thousands and took the wall down with their bare hands, dancing on it and weeping. Two million East Germans immediately went to the West, and within a year East and West Germany were reunited as a single democratic country.

Mikhail Gorbachev

In 1985 Mikhail Gorbachev, the new leader of the Union of Soviet Socialist Republics (USSR or Soviet Union), set about changing things. The republics of the USSR had been under communist rule for nearly 70 years, and had not achieved the ideal society that many early communists had hoped for. Secrecy and fear were part of daily life; people were discouraged and undernourished. Gorbachev introduced *perestroika* ('restructuring') and *glasnost* ('openness'). He wanted to bring the communist system into the modern world. He removed old-fashioned politicians from positions of power. He set about increasing agricultural production and reducing waste. He aimed to improve the national diet, cut alcohol consumption, and energize the Soviet people. He still believed in communism, and was passionate about reforming it. But the oppression of previous regimes had left many people angry.

Mikhail Gorbachev (centre) tried to reform the Communist Party in the USSR.

Mikhail Gorbachev (1931–   )

In 1980 Mikhail Gorbachev joined the communist politburo (governing body) and in 1985 he became general secretary of the Communist Party of the Soviet Union (CPSU). He set about restructuring the economy and society. He travelled around the USSR, meeting ordinary people and encouraging them to improve living standards. The restrictions of life under communism contributed towards a lot of people becoming alcoholics, and he tried to influence people to stop drinking so much. He encouraged freedom of speech and new businesses to develop. He reduced military activity abroad and developed excellent relations with Western leaders. He also agreed to remove some nuclear weapons from Europe. In 1988 he became president of the USSR. In 1991 he resigned realizing that the USSR was breaking up and that he had lost his power.

In 1988, people in the Soviet republic of Armenia demanded the return of land given by the communist dictator Joseph Stalin to the neighbouring republic of Azerbaijan. This was followed by similar demands in other Soviet republics, and violent conflicts broke out in a number of places. Too many people had been moved about and suppressed for too long – now their anger erupted. Republic after republic demanded independence, and Gorbachev began to lose control. In 1991 he was kidnapped by a group of old-style communists, but they had no real strength, and released him when he refused to negotiate. Meanwhile, Boris Yeltsin, leader of the Russian republic, became more popular and more powerful. Gorbachev resigned from the Communist Party, dismissed its central committee, and tried to work with Yeltsin, but his power was fast disappearing. Gorbachev resigned on 25 December 1991, and on the same day the USSR ceased to exist. Soviet communism in Europe was at an end.

Information Technology and the Computer Age

By the 1990s computers were used in all areas of modern society. Simple microchips controlled washing machines and video recorders. Computer-controlled robot arms that could cut, drill, weld, or paint were used on manufacturing production lines. Computers controlled everything from air-traffic networks to the National Lottery, and many people used computers both at work and at home.

Colossus, the Code-Cracking Computer

One of the earliest electronic computers was the Colossus, built in 1943 in Britain. Britain was at war, and Colossus carried out thousands of calculations in order to crack the ever-changing code used by the Germans for sending top-secret messages.

A technician enters data into 'Baby', the first computer that could be programmed.

Did You Know?

Today's small PCs are more powerful than the computers used to guide the *Apollo 11* spacecraft to the Moon in 1969.

Early Computers

The earliest computers were built in the 1940s. These were huge room-filling machines. The first general-purpose computer was ENIAC (the Electronic Numerical Integrator and Computer), built in the USA. It was probably the first machine to be called a computer. The early 1950s saw the first computers with memories, which could store programs for use again and again. Memory could also be used to store information.

Computers are used more and more in schools today. Information science will be very important in the 21st century.

A computer chip as seen under a microscope.

Transistors and Chips

In the early 1960s computers became much smaller as transistors were developed to replace the larger components used in early computers. Transistors were more compact, faster, and more reliable. Computers shrank even more with the development of the microchip, which fitted complicated electronic circuits onto a small piece of silicon crystal that was only a few millimetres square. By the 1970s the whole 'brain' of a computer could be squeezed onto one microchip.

PCs and Software

Computers could now be made small enough to fit onto a desk, and in 1975 the Altair, the first personal computer (PC), was built. The Altair used a computer language called BASIC, which was adapted for it by two men: Bill Gates and Paul Allen. In 1975 they set up a company called Microsoft to develop new computer programs, or 'software'. In the 1980s Microsoft developed 'user-friendly' software such as Windows™, which made computers easier to use. The combination of desktop computers with better software led to an explosion in the sales of personal computers.

Building the Net

Computers using different systems were first linked together in the USA in 1969. This first computer network was called the ARPANET and it joined computers at four US universities using telephone lines to make the connections. By 1972 ARPANET users were sending electronic mail (e-mail) messages to each other across the network. By the mid 1980s there were a thousand computers in the ARPANET, by 1995 there were 60,000 linked in what was now known as the Internet.

Today no one knows how many millions of people access the Internet every day. Smaller networks of computers can be linked to the world-spanning Internet through routers, 'gateway' computers that link networks together. People at home can use their personal computers and modems to link into the Internet through a service provider's gateway computer.

The Internet really began to take off commercially with the development of the World Wide Web, which allows computers to share words, pictures, and sounds easily and brought multimedia to the Internet. Today people all over the world use the Internet to send e-mails, take part in discussions, play games, buy and sell products, and get news and information.

Policing the Net

So much information is held on computers, for instance health records, bank accounts, and police files, that most countries have passed laws to stop the information being misused. Regulating information on the Internet is difficult because it is a global system with no central control.

Sport in the 20ᵗʰ Century

In the 19th century people normally played sport for pleasure and to keep fit. The birth of the modern Olympic movement in 1896 helped change the role of sport in the 20th century. Large numbers of people began to watch excellent sportsmen and sportswomen perform. Rather than just playing, people now wanted to watch and support their local teams or countries. As soon as crowds started to watch people playing, businesses and industries wanted to pay money so that they could advertise their goods to the crowds of people.

People used to listen to broadcasts of their favourite events on the radio, but when television became widely available many more people were able to watch their sporting heroes. Television also meant that companies and television networks were prepared to pay even more money to advertise at sporting events. The US television network NBC (National Broadcasting Company), for example, paid the Olympic movement billions of dollars to be able to broadcast the games in the year 2000.

By the end of the 20th century sports such as football, athletics, tennis, golf, American football, and baseball had professional organizations that were able to pay the players huge sums of money. These sports were taken very seriously, not only by those who played but also by the millions of people who paid to watch their favourite players and teams. Football teams such as Manchester United and American football teams such as the Denver Broncos attract huge groups of fans who are desperate to see them win.

Unfortunately, this pressure to win sometimes led to bad consequences. Football hooligans, groups of rival fans who behave violently, sometimes got into fights at matches. Another bad consequence was that some players became so desperate to win that they took drugs that could help them perform better.

British athlete Sally Gunnell was one of Britain's most popular sporting heros, winning medals and setting world record times as a hurdler.

Sports Stars

Some sportsmen and sportswomen are amongst the most famous people in the world. Martina Navratilova is one of the most successful tennis players of all time. Tiger Woods, the young US golf star, is now recognizable around the world. Michael Jordan, the recently retired US basketball player, has been responsible for making basketball a spectator sport worldwide. The Brazilian soccer star Ronaldo is so famous around the world that he is known by only one name!

Politics and the Olympic Games

The Nazi leader Adolf Hitler tried to use the 1936 Berlin Olympics to promote racist attitudes, including the idea that white people are always better than blacks. The black American Jesse Owens proved him wrong by winning four gold medals in track and field events.

Ten days into the 1972 Olympics in Munich, West Germany, eight members of the Black September terrorist group captured eleven Israeli athletes, starting a crisis that ended 17 hours later in the death of all the Israelis, five of the terrorists, and one German police officer. After a memorial service, the Games continued.

The opening ceremony of the 1996 Olympic games in Atlanta, USA. 5,500 athletes took part.

Pelé (1940-)

Edson Arantes do Nascimento, the Brazilian footballer known as Pelé, scored 1,281 first-class goals during his career. He won his first cap at the age of 17 at the 1958 World Cup finals in Sweden and became a veteran of four World Cups. When he retired at the age of 34, his club Santos removed the number 10 shirt from the line-up in honour of him. He is now regarded by many people as the greatest footballer of all time.

An exciting moment from the 1998 football World Cup finals.

Muhammad Ali (1942-)

Muhammad Ali is one of the 20th century's best known sportsmen. He won the Olympic light-heavyweight boxing title in 1960. When he turned professional, he became the first and only man so far to win the world heavyweight championship three times. The title was stripped from him in 1967 because he refused to be drafted into the US army. He retired from boxing in 1982.

Football World Cup Winners

1930	Uruguay	1970	Brazil
1934	Italy	1974	West Germany
1938	Italy	1978	Argentina
1950	Uruguay	1982	Italy
1954	West Germany	1986	Argentina
1958	Brazil	1990	West Germany
1962	Brazil	1994	Brazil
1966	England	1998	France

Human Rights

What is Racism?

Racists are people who dislike and think they are better than people of other races. Often racism comes from ignorance and fear of different cultures. For centuries people have used their racist beliefs to justify abuse and bad treatment of minorities. Even today, millions of people of African, Asian, and South American descent living in Europe and the USA find it far more difficult to lead their lives than the white people who live alongside them.

Nazism

The Nazi movement, founded in Germany in 1921, developed the hatred of other races as one of its main beliefs. Adolf Hitler, the Nazi leader, believed that only people of 'Aryan' (Germanic and Scandinavian) descent were proper human beings. He wanted two things – to create 'a master race' by allowing only Aryans to have children; and to acquire more land for this race to live on. In search of this land, Hitler invaded Poland and triggered World War II. During the war the Nazis imprisoned, robbed, and slaughtered 6 million Jews, as well as gypsies and members of other groups that they hated.

Martin Luther King (1929–1968)

Martin Luther King was a Baptist minister who lived in the southern USA, where there was a lot of prejudice against black people. In 1955 he was chosen as leader in a local protest against racial segregation (separation of blacks and whites). Black people refused to use buses where certain seats were reserved for whites. Bus companies lost so much money that they gave in. King supported protests in other areas. In 1963 he led over 200,000 people on a march to Washington, DC, home of the US government. There, he made a speech about a society free of racial hatred and injustice. 'I have a dream', he said 'that my four little children will one day live in a nation where they will not be judged by the colour of their skin but by the content of their character'. In 1964 he won the Nobel Peace Prize. In 1968 he was shot dead.

FOR DEMOCRACY

The Universal Declaration of Human Rights, 1948

This document included a number of important principles, including the following.

- All human beings are born free and equal and should act towards one another in a spirit of brotherhood.
- Everyone has the right to life, liberty, and security of person.
- No one shall be subjected to torture or to cruel treatment.
- Everyone has the right to education.
- Everyone has duties to the community in which the full development of his or her personality is possible.

Since Stephen Lawrence was murdered in a racist assault in London in 1993 his parents have fought without success to have his attackers brought to justice.

Aung San Suu Kyi (centre) has worked tirelessly for human rights in Myanmar in Southeast Asia. She was awarded the Nobel Peace prize in 1991 while still under house arrest.

Apartheid

In 1948 the white South African government adopted the policy of apartheid (meaning 'separateness') as the basis of its political system. This meant that black South Africans were not allowed to vote, nor were they allowed to live, work, travel, eat, or anything else you can think of alongside whites. They could work for whites, but their legal rights were so few that they were treated almost like slaves. In 1990 President F W de Klerk began to dismantle the system. In 1994, after free elections in which non-white people voted for the first time, the black leader Nelson Mandela became president of an apartheid-free South Africa.

Discrimination

Other groups, as well as racial minorities, suffer from being treated as inferior. In most societies, women are often still not treated as the equals of men. Disabled people, homosexuals, elderly people, poor people, certain religious groups, and single parents all suffer from the effects of discrimination.

The Developing World

The poorer countries of the world are mostly in Central and South America, the Caribbean, Africa, and Asia. Together these countries are often called 'developing countries' or 'less developed countries', and they contain almost three-quarters of the world's population.

What is Development?

A developed country is one that has many industries, a good network of roads and railways, and plenty of schools and hospitals for everybody. In the developing countries some or all of these things may be missing, and most of the people are very poor. Natural disasters such as droughts and floods may result in famines and epidemics of disease, as the countries may be too poor to cope with such calamities.

In many countries people are forced to scrape a living from other people's rubbish.

Mother Teresa (1910–1997)

Mother Teresa was a Roman Catholic nun who worked among the poor people of Calcutta in India. There she helped abandoned children and looked after the dying. In 1979 she was awarded the Nobel Peace Prize.

The Colonial Legacy

Nearly all the countries of the developing world were once European colonies. Although the European countries believed that they were bringing 'Western civilization' to their colonies, one of the main reasons for colonization was economic. The industrial countries of Europe needed new sources of raw materials (such as minerals, metals, and agricultural products), and also needed new markets for the manufactured goods they produced. As a result, the economies of the colonized countries were changed to suit the needs of the colonial powers. For example, many farmers stopped growing food for their own needs, and instead grew 'cash crops' for export, such as tobacco, sugar, cotton, tea, coffee, and rubber.

In the decades following World War II nearly all the countries of the developing world gained their independence, but the economic system more or less stayed in place. Many developing countries rely on exports of a small range of

International aid programmes can make a real difference to the lives of people in the developing world.

raw (natural) materials, and the prices of these materials on the world market often go down as well as up. In contrast, the prices of most of the manufactured goods that they need to import – such as medicines, tractors, and refrigerators – usually only go up. Consequently, many developing countries owe huge amounts of money to Western banks and other institutions, and have to spend much of their money on repayments rather than on development projects to help their own people.

Political Instability

When the European powers set up their colonies, some of them took little account of the people who lived there. In Africa especially, the borders of the colonies ignored tribal divisions. After independence, tension between different tribal groups in many countries led to civil war. In addition, during the period of the Cold War, both the Western powers and the Soviet Union and its allies backed different sides in various regional conflicts in the developing world. Frequent warfare has increased the poverty of many developing countries, with governments spending large amounts on arms.

Democratic government is fairly rare in the developing world. Many rulers have only kept themselves in power with the help of the army, and there are few countries where the army itself has not at some time seized power. Without stable democratic institutions, corruption in many countries has become common, with those in power taking money that would otherwise be used for development projects.

The Cost of Living: The Environment

The 20th century saw rapid advances in technology and industrial development. Our society has become wealthier as a result. In environmental terms, though, this wealth has a huge cost.

In 1962, in her book *Silent Spring,* the US biologist Rachel Carson warned that by using chemical pesticides and weedkillers, we were poisoning ourselves and our environment. Her warning was not heeded. Around the same time, the US Food and Drugs Administration noted that farm produce lacked nutritional value because there were few minerals available in the soil. The wide use of toxic chemicals had already done damage.

Chemicals poison the atmosphere. Carbon monoxide, heavy metals, and other toxins in the air damage people's health. Industrial societies are plagued by waste. Poisonous waste is dumped in the sea, buried in the ground, burnt (giving off toxic fumes), or left to decay.

Every day huge areas of rainforest are destroyed to make room for farmland.

The problem of waste disposal is becoming more and more urgent.

Organizations like Greenpeace helped in Kuwait when the oil wells were set alight at the end of the Gulf War in 1991.

European trees are dying from pollution. Meanwhile, loggers and farmers are cutting down the vast tropical forests. The loss of the forests will be terrible. They influence the world's climate and an estimated half of the world's plant and animal species live there. Animal species, are also dying out because of people hunting them.

World leaders are now working to address these problems; time is short, and they need to work fast.

The Greenhouse Effect

The term 'greenhouse effect' was invented by a Swedish scientist in 1896. He predicted it as a result of the burning of fossil fuels (chiefly coal). Greenhouse gases such as carbon dioxide, released when these fuels are burned, let the Sun's heat in, but will not let it escape from the Earth's atmosphere. The Earth's surface will then become gradually hotter. The fine balance of our global ecosystem cannot survive very much change of this sort. Already there is concern that some of the Polar ice is melting. This produces a risk of low-lying land being covered by the sea.

Nuclear Waste

Nuclear energy was developed first for use in weapons. Then it was used as a cheap source of electrical power. The materials used to produce nuclear energy are exceptionally dangerous. Nuclear waste is radioactive and the energy it releases can damage living organisms. No satisfactory way has yet been found of disposing of it. It is in storage, awaiting a solution.

The Ozone Layer

Ozone is one of the gases that make up our atmosphere. It exists in a thin layer of particles, 19 to 30 kilometres (12 to 20 miles) up off the Earth's surface. It is our only protection against the harmful effects of the Sun's ultraviolet radiation. In the 1980s, a hole was detected in the ozone layer over Antarctica. By 1991 scientists believed that one-twentieth of the layer was being lost every ten years.

Chemicals called chlorofluorocarbons – CFCs – have been identified as particularly harmful to the ozone layer. They have been used in such things as aerosol sprays and fridges. Other ozone-destroying chemicals are used in fire extinguishers, solvents, and pesticides. Their use is now being phased out.

The End of the Millennium

The 20th century has been perhaps the greatest period of change in human history. The discoveries and inventions made in the course of the last 100 years have altered the world beyond recognition.

In the first years of the 21st century the United States and the United Kingdom will both have to hold elections. The US presidential elections will take place in November 2000. President Clinton cannot by law stand again – so who will the next president be? There will have to be a General Election in the United Kingdom before May 2002. Will the first Labour government in nearly 20 years be re-elected?

On 31 December 1999, Boris Yeltsin unexpectedly resigned as president of Russia. Mr Yeltsin became the country's first democratically-elected head of state in 1991. He said that Russia needed "new politicians, new faces, new intelligent, strong and energetic people" for the new millennium. Vladimir Putin, his prime minister was appointed acting president and is the firm favourite to win the presidential elections due to be held on 26 March 2000.

Millions of people eagerly awaited the first chimes of Big Ben that rang in the new millennium.

An Uncertain World

For many people the coming century brings with it uncertainties for the future. Although many parts of the world enjoy peace and prosperity, there are unfortunately places that suffer from fighting and unrest.

- In October 1999 in Pakistan the army overthrew the government.
- At the same time United Nations peacekeeping forces were stationed in the tiny country of East Timor to oversee its administration during the transition to independence from Indonesia.
- In March 1999 NATO warplanes began a massive assault on Serbia, Yugoslavia, to force the government there to end its violence against the Albanian population of Kosovo, an area within Serbia.
- Russian forces are at war with Chechnya, which is fighting to have its self-proclaimed independence recognized by Russia and the rest of the world.

Women in a village in Chechnya weep for their loved ones, killed in a Russian bombing raid.

The Millennium Bug

At the end of the 20th century people were concerned that the world would suddenly grind to a halt if computers went haywire as the year changed from 1999 to 2000. Year 2000 coordinators from 170 nations met at the United Nations in New York to try to put together a picture of how well the world's computer systems were prepared for the new century. They expected that the turn of the year would pass in most industrialized countries with few severe problems. In the first days of the year 2000, early indications were that the Millennium Bug had not wreaked the havoc that some had feared. People wondered whether the huge sums of money that had been spent by some countries on protecting against the Bug had been really necessary.

Celebrating the Future

The first dawn of the new millennium was seen in the remote islands of the southern Pacific. Samoa was the last place on earth to enter the new millennium. People across the world marked the beginning of the 21st century. In

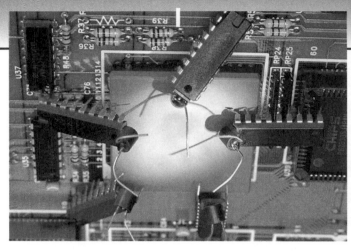

As the year 2000 drew near there were worries that computer 'bugs' might cause problems as the year changed.

London the Queen ignited a fiery beacon in the middle of the River Thames before attending the opening ceremony of the Millennium Dome. Spectacular light and firework displays were the focus for many celebrations in towns and cities across the world including London, Beijing, Moscow, Washington, Paris, and Sydney. There were candle-lit processions in Bethlehem and Jerusalem. In London the chimes of Big Ben heralded the arrival of the year 2000 as people across the land sang the traditional New Year song 'Auld Lang Syne' and, on New Year's Day, churches tolled their bells in unison in celebration of the new millennium.

The Sydney Harbour Bridge and Opera House are lit up with fireworks to welcome in the new millennium, in Sydney, Australia.

Towards the Future

Predicting the future is always an uncertain task. Which of the Norman invaders in 1066 could have predicted the shape of the United Kingdom in 1999? In 1900, at the start of the 20th century, powered flight, electronic computers, television, space travel, atomic power, and DNA were all unknowns. What does the next millennium have in store?

Gooey Future?

Children from Britain and Ireland were asked for their thoughts on the future for a book on the next millennium. Among their suggestions were that t-shirts will be made of goo, the sea will be made of hot chocolate, and cats will speak English!

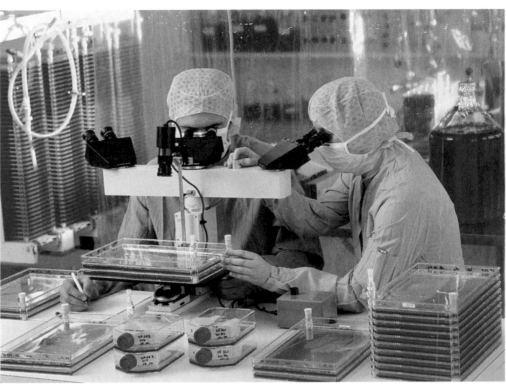

Medical research is sure to provide some of the 21st century's greatest opportunities and challenges.

The Gene Genie

In the face of public outcry against genetically modified foods the food giants such as Monsanto appear to be in retreat. It seems that, for now at least, the gene genie has been put back in its bottle. However, there is more to genetics than modifying foods.

A scientist at Cornell University in the United States of America has engineered a banana that contains a vaccine. The modified banana has cut the cost of inoculating a child in a developing country a thousand times.

In the near future a doctor might take a drop of blood or wipe the inside of your cheek to get a sample for genetic testing. The results could tell the doctor whether you are likely to get certain diseases and which will be the best drugs to prescribe to treat them.

At the beginning of the 21st century the Human Genome Project will complete its massive task of providing us with a map of all the human genes that guide the way our bodies develop from conception to death.

By 2010 doctors predict that we will have treatments for diseases that are presently incurable, such as Alzheimer's Disease. Supercomputers might be used in place of doctors to diagnose illness. A brand new computer system at Coventry University can now diagnose illness correctly more often than doctors can.

The Digital Revolution

The use of computers and digital technology in the communications industry will doubtless continue to grow. Faster connections to the Internet via cable TV links promise to lead to a future where the Internet and television blur together into one source of information and entertainment. It is possible to imagine watching a movie and calling up information about the actors in a box in the corner of the screen from an Internet link for example.

How Many More?

In 1999 the world population reached 6 billion people. By the end of the next century there may be 12 billion people struggling to find room on a crowded planet. Population growth is sharply divided across the world. In developing countries the average age can be as young as 15 and the growth rate is fast enough to double the population in 23 years. In the rich, developed world on the other hand the average age in countries like Japan is much older and the population growth in those countries has fallen to almost zero or below, meaning that the number of people in these countries may actually be falling. The United Nations predicts that in 2050 a quarter of the developed world's people will be older than 65.

As the human family grows in number we have to find ways of living together peaceably so that everyone has hope for the future.

Water and Warming

By 2050, according to some estimates, a quarter of the world will have less water than it needs.

In places such as the Middle East wars might be fought for control of scarce drinking water. Global warming may also cause problems. Some scientists predict that the sea level could rise by as much as a metre over the next century.

New Worlds

NASA scientists believe that someone from Earth will walk on the surface of Mars sometime in the early 21st century. Unmanned spacecraft are currently surveying the Red Planet, as Mars is known, and are gathering information about what will be needed to send people to Mars. This could happen as early as 2012. In 2005 scientists plan to send a vehicle to pick up rock samples from the surface of Mars and then launch them back into space to arrive on Earth by 2008.

Spaceprobes such as the *Mars Pathfinder* are blazing a trail to the planets that people may follow one day soon.

Index

Picture Acknowledgements

t = top, b = bottom, l = left, r = right, c = centre

4–7 et archive; 8 Popperfoto; 9 et archive; 10 Tretyakov Gallery, Moscow/Bridgeman Art Library; 11 t AKG London, b Institute of Slavonic Studies/et archive; 12 AKG London; 13 t Hulton Getty; b AKG London; 14 Popperfoto; 15 et archive; 16 t © Salvador Dali–Foundation Gala–Salvador Dali/DACS 2000/AKG London, b The Andy Warhol Foundation for the Visual Arts, inc./ARS, NY and DACS, London 2000/Estate of Marilyn Monroe licensed by CMG Worldwide, Inc./Tate Gallery, London/et archive; 17 l Angelo Hornak, r Keith Collie/AKG London; 18 Illustration from THE TALE OF BENJAMIN BUNNY by Beatrix Potter. Copyright © by Frederick Warne & Co., 1904, 1987. Reproduced by kind permission of Frederick Warne & Co; 19 t © DC Thompson/et archive; 19 b–20 t Rex, 20 b AKG London; 21 Rex; 22 AKG London/AP; 23 t Alfred Pasieka/Science Photo Library, b AEA Technology; 24 t Popperfoto, b AKG London; 25 Hulton Getty; 26 Popperfoto; 27 AKG London; 28 t Imperial War Museum/et archive, b et archive; 29 AKG London; 31 t Imperial War Museum/et archive, 31 b–32 Popperfoto; 33 AKG London; 34 t Imperial War Museum/et archive, 34 b–35 Popperfoto; 36 t Library of Congress/et archive, b French Railways; 37 et archive; 38 t AKG London, b Rex; 39 Corbis; 40 t Mark Henley/Impact, b AKG London; 41 Department of Clinical Radiology, Salisbury District Hospital/Science Photo Library; 42 Ronald Grant; 43 AKG London; 44 Mark Henley/Impact; 45 AKG London; 46 John Cole/Impact; 47 Rex; 48 t Popperfoto, b Rex; 49 AKG London; 50 et archive; 51 t Popperfoto, b Rex; 52 Hulton Getty; 53 t James Fraser/Impact, b Rex; 54 t Mary Evans Picture Library, b Corbis; 55 t AKG London, b Rex; 56 Corbis-Bettmann; 57 t Adam Hart-Davis/Science Photo Library, b David Ducros/Science Photo Library; 58 Mary Evans Picture Library; 59 Rex; 60 Popperfoto; 61 t Corbis-Bettmann, b Popperfoto; 62–63 AKG London; 64 Hulton Getty; 65 t Rex, b Reuters/Corbis-Bettmann; 66–68 Rex; 69 t Pacemaker Press, b Rex; 70 NASA/Science Photo Library; 71 NASA; 73 t Bruce Stephens/Impact, b Philip Gordon/Impact; 74–75 Rex; 76 t James King-Holmes/Science Photo Library, b Chris Moyse/Impact; 77 Michael W Davidson/Science Photo Library; 78–79 c Rex, 79 b AKG London; 80 UPI/Corbis-Bettmann; 81 t–82 l Rex, 82 r Daniel White/Impact; 83 Caroline Penn/Impact; 84 t Colin Jones/Impact, b Bruce Stephens/Impact; 85 Rex; 86 t Joe Cornish/Tony Stone, b Frank Spooner Pictures; 87 t Larry Gilpin/Tony Stone, b AP Photos/Russell McPhedran; 88 Michael Rosenfeld/Tony Stone; 89 t Ken Fisher/Tony Stone, b NASA.

Cover illustrations (clockwise from top right):
Illustration from THE TALE OF BENJAMIN BUNNY by Beatrix Potter. Copyright © by Frederick Warne & Co., 1904, 1987. Reproduced by kind permission of Frederick Warne & Co; Keith Collie/AKG London; Rex; Reuters/Corbis-Bettmann; AKG London; NASA.

Every effort has been made to give the correct acknowledgement for each picture. However, should there be any inaccuracy or omission, we would be pleased to insert the correct acknowledgement in a future edition or printing of this volume.